Galileo Galilei

First Physicist

GALILEO GALILEI LINCEO FILOSOFO E MATEMATICO DEL SER.^{mo} GRAN DVCA DI TOSCA

F. Villamœna Fecit.

Owen Gingerich
General Editor

Galileo Galilei

First Physicist

James MacLachlan

Oxford University Press
New York • Oxford

Fondly dedicated to the memory of
Stillman Drake (1910–1993) extraordinary scholar
of Galileo and unselfish friend

Oxford University Press

Oxford New York
Athens Auckland Bangkok Bogotá Bombay
Buenos Aires Calcutta Cape Town Dar es Salaam
Delhi Florence Hong Kong Istanbul Karachi
Kuala Lumpur Madras Madrid Melbourne
Mexico City Nairobi Paris Singapore
Taipei Tokyo Toronto Warsaw
and associated companies in
Berlin Ibadan

Copyright © 1997 by James MacLachlan
Published by Oxford University Press, Inc.,
198 Madison Avenue, New York, New York 10016
Website: www.opu-usa.org
First issued as an Oxford University Press paperback in 1999

Oxford is a registered trademark of Oxford University Press

Design: Design Oasis
Layout: Leonard Levitsky
Picture research: Lisa Kirchner

Library of Congress Cataloging-in-Publication Data
MacLachlan, James
Galileo Galilei: first physicist / James MacLachlan.
p. cm. — (Oxford portraits in science)
Includes bibliographical references and index.
ISBN 0-19-509342-9 (library edition); ISBN 0-19-513170-3 (paperback)
1. Galilei, Galileo, 1564-1642—Biography—Juvenile literature.
2. Physicists—Italy—Biography—Juvenile literature.
[1. Galileo, 1564-1642. 2. Scientists.]
I. Title. II. Series.
QC16.G35M33   1996
520'.92—dc20   95-45028
                                  CIP
9 8 7 6 5 4

Printed in the United States of America
on acid-free paper

On the cover: *Galileo in 1624* Inset: *The earliest known portrait of Galileo,*
  done around 1603.

Frontispiece: *A portrait of Galileo by Francesco Villamena.*

YB
GAL

Contents

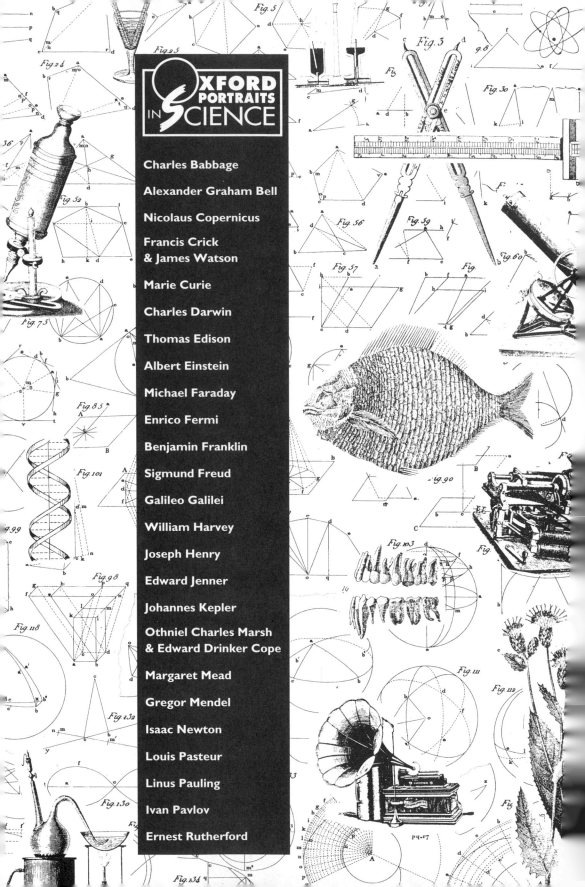

OXFORD
PORTRAITS
IN SCIENCE

And new Philosophy calls all in doubt,
The Element of fire is quite put out;
The Sun is lost, and th'earth, and no man's wit
Can well direct him where to look for it.
John Donne, *An Anatomy of the World* (1611)

Go, Wondrous creature! mount where science guides;
Go, measure earth, weigh air, and state the tides;
Instruct the planets in what orbs to run,
Correct old time and regulate the Sun;
Alexander Pope, *An Essay on Man* (1733)

The Science of Physics

Until the 1600s, people treated many kinds of knowledge as aspects of philosophy. They used general principles of reasoning to explain nature, society, and religion. Then Galileo and others developed new methods for examining the world of nature. By adding experimenting, measuring, and calculating to reasoning, they took the study of nature out of philosophy and turned it into science.

Today we recognize branches of science such as biology, chemistry, and physics. Each of them has a different focus: life for biology, materials for chemistry, actions and forces for physics. But despite their different focuses, these sciences share many techniques. Galileo's work in physics helped greatly to make experimental measurements and mathematical calculations more prominent in all the sciences.

Taking his cue from the methods of astronomers, Galileo began to study nature on earth by using methods of measuring and calculating still used today. He applied these methods mainly in his study of motions: falling stones and swinging pendulums, among others. He also made important discoveries in astronomy, using a telescope that he improved significantly soon after it was invented in 1608.

Physics is the Greek word for nature. Twenty-three hundred years ago, the Athenian philosopher Aristotle wrote a book on natural philosophy, which he entitled *Physics*. Aristotle's views of nature dominated European thought for almost 2,000 years. Natural philosophers taught a set of precepts about the causes of all earthly actions and the nature of the whole universe. They did no measuring, performed no experiments, and made few calculations. Galileo found their explanations of motion unconvincing. He was particularly dissatisfied because Aristotle had concentrated on *why* objects move. Galileo wanted to know *how* they move.

Galileo transformed Aristotle's logic of nature into mathematical, experimental physics. However, for more than a hundred years the English-speaking world continued to call it natural philosophy. In France before the end of the 1600s, the experimental-mathematical study of nature was called *la physique*. The scholars engaged in these studies were called *physiciens* (physicists). The English word *physicist* was not coined until 1840. Although Galileo was not called a physicist in his own time, his work provided procedures and results that lie at the heart of what we know today as physics.

Galileo was born in Pisa, home to the famed Leaning Tower, in 1564.

Young Mathematician

The young man waited impatiently. After all, it was his future they were deciding—the rest of his life. He paced nervously as his father and the grand duke's mathematician argued behind closed doors. They just had to let him study mathematics.

The crisis had come to a head in the spring of 1584. Galileo Galilei, aged 20, was attending the University of Pisa, studying philosophy and medicine in order to become a doctor. At least that is what he was supposed to be studying. Recently, however, his father, Vincenzio Galilei, had learned that his son was neglecting his regular studies. Instead, Galileo was concentrating all his energies on mathematics. The grand duke's mathematician, Ostillio Ricci, had lent him mathematical texts by Euclid and Archimedes (Greek masters of 2,000 years earlier). The youth had found them much more intriguing than the dry-as-dust works of those other Greeks: Aristotle on philosophy and Galen on medicine.

Vincenzio had made the 60-mile trip from Florence solely to confront his son, so Galileo was understandably relieved when Ricci volunteered to intervene with his furious father. Vincenzio was sure the family fortunes hung on the income Galileo would earn as a doctor. Mathematicians, by comparison, had to be content with a mere pittance.

Ricci finally persuaded Vincenzio that Galileo had real talent in mathematics. Lacking any inspiration for medicine, he would probably not make much of a doctor anyway. They called Galileo in. Vincenzio grudgingly agreed to continue his son's support for another year. After that, he would be on his own. Galileo was overjoyed. No longer would he have to pretend to be studying medicine rather than mathematics. Soon, he would be adding to the fund of mathematical knowledge. Already he thought he could improve on the theorem of levers proposed by the esteemed Greek mathematician Archimedes in the third century B.C. He would show his father. Maybe a really good mathematician could become as famous as any local doctor. Maybe more famous!

The century of Galileo's birth saw many changes in Europe. By 1500, Europeans were beginning to expand westward with Columbus to the Americas and eastward with Vasco da Gama to the fabled riches of Asia. With their cannons and tall ships they plundered the wealth of the Indies. In 1522, Ferdinand Magellan's ships returned from the first round-the-world tour.

Expanding trade enriched the monarchs of western Europe and gave them more power. Greedy for still more influence, they sought to diminish the control of the pope and the Catholic Church. Kings in Spain and France won the right to appoint their own bishops. When the Church refused him a divorce, Henry VIII of England used the occasion to confiscate the monasteries and remove the English church from the control of the pope in Rome.

Central Europe at the time was a loose confederation of Germanic states under the Holy Roman Emperor in Prague. The emperor belonged to the same dynasty as the king of Spain.

Princes of the northern German states adopted Martin Luther's Protestant Reformation to increase their local power. Initially, Luther had only wanted to eliminate religious abuses stemming from the supreme authority of the pope. But he came to feel that people's contact with God should be direct, needing no mediation by priests. In the 1520s, Luther split from the Roman Catholic Church and established one of his own. He believed that the core of religious faith came from the Bible, not from church councils and officials. Luther also promoted nationalism by translating the New Testament into German. In response, the Catholic Church undertook reforms of its own. The Council of Trent (1545–63) reconfirmed its basic doctrines, while correcting numerous faults in church government.

In 1540, the Catholic Church established a new religious community, the Society of Jesus. Expanding rapidly in numbers, the black-robed Jesuits opened more than 100 new colleges across Europe before 1600. They taught modern views of geography and history in place of the traditional Latin classics, along with rigorous adherence to Catholic beliefs. Eventually some Protestants thought highly enough of Jesuit education to send their children to Jesuit schools.

Education at this time was mostly confined to urban areas. In some Italian cities, as many as 40 percent of girls and boys received elementary schooling. However, until after 1800, no more than about 15 percent of Europe's population lived in towns and cities.

Both education and nationalism were greatly enhanced by mechanical printing. Between 1450 and 1500, printing presses had spread to more than 200 towns in Europe. The printing industry more than doubled in the following hundred years. Printed books cost about one-fifth as much as hand-lettered ones. Printing made an impact on society fully as great as computers have in our own day.

Printers soon exhausted their sources of traditional literature, religious tracts, and the Latin classics. They demanded new works. Men like Luther and the Jesuits happily supplied them. Reports of all the new geographical discoveries also appeared in print.

Even before 1500, another novelty had swept over Europe. Beginning in Italy, artists and sculptors created images more natural than those of their predecessors. People at the time viewed this Renaissance as a return to the purity of ancient Greece. They wrote more elegantly and added many social themes to the traditional religious ones. Their work survived because of the new printing presses.

The new authors frequently wrote in their national languages rather than in the traditional Latin. This allowed education to expand since children could learn to read more quickly in their native tongue than in the foreign language, Latin. However, reading in their own language made people pay more attention to their national differences. While printing broadened horizons on the one hand, it narrowed them on the other.

Finally, although Europe was becoming modern, it did so slowly. Transportation was still limited to the speed a person or a horse could walk or a ship could sail. And while most clothing was still made at home of local farm products, factory production of textiles was increasing in many towns. Spinners and weavers worked at primitive wooden machines.

Nobles who owned the textile factories became very wealthy. The Medici family in Florence used their wealth to become bankers and moneylenders to royalty. One branch of the family became the rulers of Florence. Since they also ruled the surrounding territory of Tuscany, they were called the grand dukes of Tuscany.

In Galileo's lifetime, various authorities ruled different parts of the Italian peninsula. Tuscany occupied the northwestern part, including Florence, Siena, and Pisa, which was near the coast. East and south of Tuscany, the pope in

South-central Europe in the 16th century.

Rome ruled the Papal States, including Rome and Bologna. South of the Papal States, the kingdom of Naples was ruled by Spain. North and west of Tuscany, the duke of Milan ruled a territory that stretched to the Alps. East of Milan, the republic of Venice dominated the northern end of the Adriatic Sea.

Three-quarters of Europe's people were farmers. Few cities had populations as great as 100,000. Infant mortality was often as high as 20 percent. More than a third of the population was under 14 years of age. People who survived their first year could expect to live on average to 45. Only about 5 percent of the population lived to 65 or beyond. Besides the ordinary causes of death, people (especially in the towns) lived in fear of recurrent bubonic plague, the Black Death. In 1630–31, Venice lost a third of its population to plague, while Milan lost half. That is the kind of world Galileo knew.

Vincenzio Galilei came from a once-prominent family in Florence. He earned a modest living teaching music and playing his lute for wealthy patrons. In 1562, while living in Pisa, he married Giulia Ammannati. He was 42; she was 24. Their first child, Galileo, was born on February 15, 1564. They gave him the name of the famous ancestor after whom the family itself was named. Of five or six later children, only three survived infancy.

When Galileo was eight, his parents returned to Florence, leaving him in Pisa to be cared for by an aunt and uncle. He rejoined his parents two years later. After some basic education in Florence, Galileo studied the Latin classics at a monastery at Vallombrosa in the hills 20 miles east of the city. He also became proficient in drawing and in playing the lute.

Attracted by the peaceful life in the monastery, Galileo began to study for the priesthood. His father, however, had other plans for him. Having a meager income, Vincenzio wished his son to become a doctor so that he could support the family. He withdrew Galileo from the monastery at age 15. Two years later, he enrolled him at the University of Pisa in the program for arts and medicine. Galileo returned to Pisa in September 1581 to live with his aunt and uncle.

In those days, universities trained men (no women were enrolled) for the three professions of theology, law, and medicine. However, along with their professional training, all students had to study philosophy. Studies in philosophy concentrated mainly on the writings of Aristotle. This Greek of the third century B.C. had produced a number of works that covered the knowledge of his time. Around 1300, scholars such as Thomas Aquinas revised parts of Aristotle's writings to conform to Christian teachings. They then became the foundation for university studies for more than 300 years.

Aristotle had constructed a system of thought to explain and relate all of human experience. Through lectures and reading, Galileo and his fellow students had Aristotle's ideas drummed into their heads. Aristotle intended his system to be

logical and coherent. He related things in very narrow categories. For example, he attributed the activities of life to souls. Plants, wrote Aristotle, have vegetative souls that account for their growth. Animals grow by their vegetative souls and also have animate souls that account for their ability to move. Finally, according to Aristotle, humans have the capacity for thinking because they have rational souls in addition to their vegetative and animate ones.

A scene from Galileo's youth: Pisa, near the mouth of the Arno River.

Aristotle founded his logic on simple general deductions: All men are mortal. Socrates is a man. Therefore, Socrates is mortal. To explain the structure of the universe, Aristotle made a radical distinction between the earth and the heavens. He put the earth in the center, with the moon, sun, planets, and stars orbiting in spheres centered on the earth. For him, the heavens were perfect and eternal, turning in perfectly circular orbits, and composed of a special celestial material, called *aether* in Greek.

By contrast, the earth and its surroundings out to the moon were the scene of constant change. Materials in the earthly realm consisted of varying mixtures of the four elements—earth, water, air, and fire. Aristotle "deduced" these elements from properties of heat and moisture: earth is cold and dry, water is cold and wet, air is hot and wet, and fire is hot and dry.

All the changes in the earthly realm required causes. Aristotle proposed four causes, which he illustrated by the example of making a statue of the Greek goddess Athena. To make it you need the material cause, the marble. You also need the formal cause, the shape or form of the goddess. The sculptor with his tools provides the efficient cause, the activity of making the statue. And the purpose for which the statue is intended—worship or decoration—is the final cause.

These ideas and many more formed the philosophical system that Galileo studied in his courses at Pisa. They provided the framework for knowing the world that was the common property of educated people all across Europe. And they had the support of the authority of the churches, both Catholic and Protestant.

Galileo, however, resisted accepting these ideas merely on the say-so of dull professors and an old Greek who had died 2,000 years earlier. In this, Galileo followed the example of his father, who was involved in arguments about music theory. Vincenzio wrote an important book contradicting the traditional theories of music.

Music theory also came from the ancient Greeks. They said that harmonious sounds from a lute depended on the lengths of the strings being simple fractions of one another. For example, the octave ratio is 1:2 (meaning that a string an octave above another is half as long), the fifth is 2:3, and the fourth is 3:4. On no account, they said, can you expect harmony if the string lengths are related by fractions with numbers much larger than that.

As a proficient lutenist, Vincenzio Galilei claimed that harmony should be determined by what pleases our ears. He performed experiments with string lengths and tensions, and he produced harmonies that were not limited to fractions of only small integers. When tensions were in the ratio of 16:25, for example, the notes were perfectly harmonious. Vincenzio's attitude of attending to real experience rather than oversimplified theory also influenced his son.

Galileo's father, Vincenzio, was an excellent lutenist, like the one shown here accompanying an organist.

In late winter of 1583, Galileo discovered a route to learning much more appealing than Aristotle's—the logic of the geometry of Euclid. Mathematics entered only slightly in the curriculum of the Faculty of Arts and Medicine. But it was being taught more fully to the pages at the Tuscan court. Each year the grand duke and his retinue spent the period between Christmas and Easter in Pisa. Although the court mathematician, Ricci, was an acquaintance of Galileo's father, Vincenzio had kept Galileo from mathematics because he considered that it oppressed music theory.

In Pisa, away from his father, Galileo visited Ricci at the court and discovered the mathematics of Euclid. Euclid's geometry had been the standard textbook of mathematics since he wrote it in Alexandria in about 300 B.C. Galileo was impressed by its compelling logic. He may well have felt as Thomas Hobbes did 45 years later. Hobbes was an important English philosopher whose first introduction to mathematics came by chance, long after his formal education had ended. Hobbes's reaction was recorded in a contemporary sketch of his life:

> He was 40 years old before he saw any Geometry, and it happened by accident. Waiting in a gentleman's library one day, Hobbes saw Euclid's Elements lying open at the Pythagorean theorem (Book 1, Proposition 47). He read the statement of the theorem. By G—, he said (from time to time he would swear for emphasis) *this is impossible!* So he read the theorem through, and found it referred him

back to earlier ones; which he also read. And so on, until at
last he was thoroughly convinced of the truth of the original theorem. That made him in love with Geometry.

Hobbes fell so much in love with geometry that 20
years later he was made mathematical tutor to the Prince of
Wales (later Charles II). Galileo, similarly, tutored the heir
to the grand duchy of Tuscany in mathematics about 20
years after his own first encounter with geometry.

Galileo took some instruction from Ricci and then
borrowed books to continue on his own. Before long he
was devoting all his energies to the study of geometry.
Ricci also introduced him to the writings of Archimedes,
widely acknowledged to be the greatest mathematician of
ancient times. From Archimedes Galileo learned how to
apply geometrical reasoning to concrete objects like levers
and floating bodies.

After winning his father's grudging support to continue
in mathematics, Galileo stayed on in Pisa until the spring of
1585. Then, having neglected his regular studies, Galileo
skipped the final exams, and left the university without a
degree. He then set out to earn his living as a mathematician. Occasionally, he managed to find brief stints as a pri-
vate tutor. The rest of the time, he continued to study the
work of Archimedes and began to look for ways to extend
the ideas he learned from the Greek mathematician. Soon
he had devised a theorem to improve the calculations used
to find the centers of gravity of solids. An object balances
on its center of gravity. The calculation of the location of
the center of gravity of a complicated shape is a robust
mathematical problem.

Galileo sent his theorem to several mathematicians to
win their approval and support. One of these was a nobleman in Urbino named Guidobaldo del Monte. His brother
was a cardinal prominent in the affairs of Florence.
Recognizing Galileo's talents, they sought positions for him
to teach mathematics full-time.

Galileo traveled to Rome in the fall of 1587 to meet the chief mathematician of the Roman College (*Collegio Romano*), the Jesuits' paramount training center. This man, Christoph Clavius, was renowned for his work in creating the Gregorian calendar. Back in 1582, the Church, under Pope Gregory XIII, had revised the calendar to conform more closely to the actual length of a year. The number of leap years was decreased slightly and 10 days were omitted from October 1582. Clavius, too, was impressed by Galileo, and he wrote letters of recommendation for him.

Eventually, in the fall of 1589, Galileo's sponsors managed to get him appointed to teach mathematics back at the University of Pisa. Four years after leaving without a degree, he belonged to the same staff as his old professors. But he earned only 60 florins a year, while philosophy professors earned 600 or more. In modern terms, if a prominent university professor earns $100,000, Galileo's pay would amount to only $10,000.

Galileo's teaching duties were not heavy. In his spare time, he began to try to apply the methods of Archimedes to the study of moving bodies. Aristotle had said that the weight of an object was what caused it to fall. And therefore, he argued, a heavy object would fall faster than a lighter one. Galileo observed that this theory contradicted experience. Though he admitted there was some difference in objects' rates of falling, he thought that it resulted from the buoyancy of the air. Galileo was thus extending Archimedes' ideas about the buoyancy of water.

According to Archimedes, water supports objects made of materials less dense than water. Galileo reasoned that air, too, provides some support for objects of small density. So he said that less dense objects would fall more slowly in air than denser ones. Density, not weight, was the controlling factor. Galileo even went so far as to claim that if there were no air, all objects would fall at the same rate.

Galileo was as contentious as a professor as he had been as a student. He argued against the hoary Aristotelian traditions of his former professors. In 1591, one of them, Francesco Buonamici, published a 1,000-page tome on motion. It gave every conceivable argument about the causes of motion. "Wordy, wordy, wordy," Galileo decided.

During his time in Pisa, Galileo recorded his own ideas in an essay titled *On Motion*. Though he revised it several times, he was dissatisfied with the fact that some of his theories did not match experience very closely. He did not publish the essay, hoping that some day he would find out how to improve the theories. In the 23 chapters of its final form, Galileo attacked Aristotle's theory of falling bodies and presented his own Archimedean version. He examined motion by methods that were significantly more mathematical than Buonamici's had been. But ultimately, Galileo found that the results of his deductions did not conform to actual tests.

One test that he probably performed did at least contradict Aristotle. The Leaning Tower of Pisa gains some of its fame from the idea that Galileo dropped weights from the top of this 180-foot-high bell tower. Although many present-day historians are inclined to doubt that the event ever occurred, there is evidence to suggest that Galileo performed at least one test from the tower.

An account appears in his last book, *Two New Sciences* (1638). There, Galileo described dropping iron weights from a great height. If one weight is 10 times heavier than the other (say, a cannonball of 10 pounds and a musketball of 1 pound), Aristotle said that by the time the heavier object reached the ground, the lighter would have passed

In 1591, one of Galileo's former professors, Francesco Buonamici, wrote On Motion, *a massive philosophical work.*

FRANCISCI
Bonamici Florentini
E PRIMO LOCO PHILOSOPHIAM
ordinariam in Almo Gymnasio Pisano Profitentis,

DE MOTV LIBRI X.
QVIBVS GENERALIA NATVRALIS PHILOSOPHIAE
principia summo studio collecta continentur.
NECNON VNIVERSAE QVAESTIONES AD LIBROS
De Physico auditu, de Cœlo, de Ortu, & Interitu
pertinentes explicantur.
MVLTA ITEM ARISTOTELIS LOCA EXPLANANTVR,
& Graecorum, Averrois, aliorumq́; doctorum sententia ad Theses
Peripateticas diriguntur.
ACCESSIT INDEX CAPITVM, RERVM, MEMORABILIVM.
AD FERDINANDVM MEDICEM MAGNVM
Etruriæ Ducem Serenissimum.

EX SVPERIORVM CONSENSV.

FLORENTIAE,
Apud Bartholomæum Sermartellium.
MDXCI.

only one-tenth the distance. Galileo claimed to have observed the two objects landing together—or at least being within a hand's span of each other at the end.

There is no evidence that this trial was a public display. Galileo performed it for his own satisfaction, perhaps with a few students. Nonetheless, we may imagine him taunting the philosophers: "If you don't believe me, try it for yourselves." Dragging weights to the top of a tower would not have seemed to them to be part of proper philosophizing.

Earning a tenth or less of what the philosophers did, Galileo was definitely on the bottom rung of the academic ladder, and contradicting Aristotle did not put him in good favor with his colleagues. When his three-year contract came up for renewal, he expected that it would not be renewed. He was right.

When Vincenzio Galilei died in July 1591, the load of family responsibility fell on his son. Besides the general expenses of housing and feeding the family, Galileo had a further financial burden. His sister Virginia had married early in 1591 and had to be provided with a dowry. In the custom of the times, a woman had to bring fabrics and money into her new household. Even before his father's death, Galileo had contributed a set of silken bed curtains to Virginia's dowry. As he wrote to his father, "I am now having silk fringes made to ornament the curtains, and could also have the bedstead made.... If you wish, I could also bring enough material to make four or five vests of damask and velvet of an exquisite design."

Once the cost of the dowry was negotiated, terms of payment were worked out. The total could amount to several years' salary. It would take Galileo many years to pay this debt. Galileo was in dire need of a new appointment. With the support of his aristocratic friends, he was finally able to obtain the post of mathematics professor at the University of Padua, with a salary more than double what he had been making. Things were looking up.

Aristotle claimed that heavy objects fall faster than lighter ones. Philosophers in Galileo's time still believed that. But Galileo said he came to doubt this belief in his youth by watching hailstones. He saw different-sized hailstones hitting the ground at the same time, and he decided they were falling at the same speed. He just could not believe that if they fell at different speeds, they would always start off at just the right times and places to land together.

In his essay *On Motion,* Galileo gave an argument in support of the idea that objects of different weights fall at the same rate—that is, that their speed of falling does not depend on their weight.

Consider two blocks of lead of different weights, say 1 pound and 5 pounds. Drop them from a height of 100 feet. Followers of Aristotle would say that when the heavier block hit the ground, the lighter one would only have fallen 20 feet. They fall at speeds determined by their weights.

Galileo asked, what would Aristotle determine the speed of fall to be if the two blocks were tied together? Probably he would say the 1–pound block holds back the 5–pound block. Then the two combined would fall more slowly than the 5–pound block by itself. But the combination weighs 6 pounds. By Aristotle's rule, therefore, it ought to fall faster than the 5–pound block. Faster or slower? There's a contradiction!

Galileo wrote:

> What clearer proof do we need of the error of Aristotle's opinion? Who, I ask, will not recognize the truth at once, looking at the matter simply and naturally? For, if we suppose the two blocks equal and close together, all agree they will fall with equal speed. Now, imagine them joining together while falling. Why should they double their speed as Aristotle claimed?
>
> Therefore, there is no reason why blocks of the same material but of different weights should fall at unequal rates.

Galileo did allow for shape or density to affect the rate of fall through air. Later in his life he claimed that a lock of wool and a piece of lead would fall together in a vacuum. With vacuum pumps, invented about 1650, scientists demonstrated the truth of Galileo's claim.

On August 2, 1971, *Apollo 15* astronaut David R. Scott performed this test on the moon, and the experiment was broadcast live on TV. As the camera rolled, viewers on earth saw a feather and a hammer falling side by side to the surface of the airless moon. Colonel Scott remarked, "This proves that Mr. Galileo was correct."

Professor at Padua

Padua, the leading university of Italy, attracted students from all over Europe. Compared to Padua, Pisa was a rural backwater. Though they were ruled from Venice, 25 miles to the east at the head of the Adriatic Sea, Paduans thrived on intellectual freedom. Galileo began to teach at the University of Padua in December 1592. At 28, he entered into what he later claimed were the best 18 years of his life. He found colleagues worthy of his active mind and formed several important, lifelong friendships.

Paolo Sarpi, a scholarly member of a small order of Catholic priests, advised the Venetian government in matters of politics and theology. In particular, he worked strenuously to support Venice's struggle to be free from the power of the pope. Galileo became a good friend of Sarpi's very soon after his arrival in Padua. The two frequently discussed Galileo's scientific discoveries.

A young Venetian aristocrat, Giovanfrancesco Sagredo, studied with Galileo in Padua. They remained in close contact until Sagredo died in 1620. Later, Galileo immortalized him as a character in his two greatest books.

Galileo taught mathematics for 18 years at the University of Padua, which was founded in 1238.

The philosopher Cesare Cremonini became a close friend to Galileo during his time in Padua.

Benedetto Castelli, a member of the Benedictine order, studied with Galileo in Padua from 1604 to 1607. Later in Florence, they collaborated on several scientific investigations.

Among Galileo's colleagues at the university was the prominent philosopher Cesare Cremonini. Despite Galileo's mistrust of philosophy, these two became good friends and occasionally lent each other money. Cremonini staunchly upheld all of Aristotle's teachings. He ignored the revisions made by various church fathers to force philosophy to conform to biblical teachings. Cremonini claimed that his only task was to understand what Aristotle had written. This got him into difficulty with church authorities, who ordered the Roman Inquisition, a church court charged with preserving the purity of the Christian faith, to investigate him. His independence of mind greatly appealed to Galileo, even when the two disagreed most violently.

At the University of Padua, Galileo taught mathematics and the simpler parts of astronomy. The main purpose of his courses was to provide doctors with the skills needed to cast horoscopes. To cast a horoscope, you have to calculate the exact positions of the planets at the moment of the person's birth. Which "houses" (signs of the zodiac) the planets occupied was supposed to foretell the person's life. At that time, doctors thought it was useful to know what the stars foretold of their patients' lives. If a doctor found that his patient's horoscope predicted an early death, he could be more relaxed about the treatment because it would be ultimately useless.

Instruction in mathematics was confined to the first and fifth of the 13 books of Euclid's *Elements*. Some of the basic theorems include the following: The sum of the interior angles of a triangle equals the sum of two right angles. Triangles with equal bases and heights have equal areas, no matter what their tilt. In a right-angled triangle, the square of the hypotenuse (the side of the triangle opposite the right angle) is equal to the sum of the squares of the other two sides.

In astronomy, Galileo alternated teaching the *Sphere* of Johannes Sacrobosco (meaning "John of Holy Wood") with the *Theory of the Planets* by Georg Peurbach. The *Sphere*, dating from about 1240, was a simple introduction to the cosmology of Aristotle. It described the geometrical relations among the heavenly spheres of the planets and stars. It also contained arguments that the earth was a sphere, and gave the principles of elementary timekeeping and the various climatic regions of the earth. *Theory of the Planets* described the movement across the sky of the planets and the geometric models that could be used to predict those movements.

Galileo's yearly salary in Padua was 180 florins. When his contract was renewed in 1599, it was increased to 320, and in 1606 to 520 florins. Out of these funds Galileo had to support himself and his family back in Florence. He was also still in debt for about 1,000 florins for his sister Virginia's dowry. Galileo's younger sister, Livia, married Taddeo Galletti in 1601. Her dowry added yet another burden. Galileo borrowed 600 florins for the down payment and contracted to pay Galletti 200 florins a year for five years—more than half his annual salary.

To supplement his income Galileo leased a large house. There he boarded students and taught them privately. These young aristocrats had interests beyond academic studies. Soon they would return home to take charge of their estates. Galileo taught them practical mathematical subjects such as

Galileo used his geometric and military compass to measure angles and make calculations.

surveying and how to fortify their castles. In good years, he was able to enhance his income to nearly 1,000 florins.

In the years from 1595 to 1602 Galileo worked on projects in practical mathematics. For example, he improved an existing instrument and turned it into a useful mechanical calculating device, a proportional compass. Galileo called it his geometric and military compass. The compass consists of two hinged flat arms, each about a foot long and an inch wide. Lines scribed on the arms are divided according to various arithmetic and geometric rules. To use the compass for calculations, you set the width of a pair of dividers to a length along one scale. Then you open the arms of the compass so that matching points on the two arms are the dividers' distance apart. Then you reset the dividers across another pair of matching numbers on the arms. That setting on the dividers gives the answer to the problem. Fitting a 90-degree arc between the arms turns the instrument in to a square for establishing right angles. Graduations along the arc permit its use as a sighting instrument for measuring angles.

Galileo hired a live-in artisan, Marcantonio Mazzoleni, to construct the compasses for sale. Over a period of 10 years, Mazzoleni made an average of about one compass a month. The instruments themselves brought no significant profit. Galileo's earnings came mostly from the course of instruction he offered to train purchasers in using the compass. Eventually he produced an instruction booklet in which he described more than 30 kinds of calculations.

Galileo also produced a brief treatise on mechanical devices and taught it at the university. In the treatise,

Galileo explained that machines make it possible to raise a large weight with a force less than is needed to lift the weight directly. The six machines of classical antiquity were the lever, pulley, inclined plane, wedge, screw, and wheel and axle (also called windlass, capstan, or crank). Many treatises on machines had been written before Galileo. His patron, Guidobaldo del Monte, had contributed one. Galileo applied his talents to combining the analysis of all six machines into a single simple principle.

Consider a familiar example. Anna, weighing 50 pounds, sits on one side of a seesaw, while her older brother Bruno, who weighs 150 pounds, sits on the other end. Anna can balance Bruno if she is 6 feet from the pivot and Bruno is only 2 feet from it. What Galileo pointed out was that to raise Bruno 1 foot, Anna will have to descend 3 feet. While her smaller weight does move him, she has to move three times as far to do it. Galileo described a similar situation in the following terms (assuming that Anna could actually lift her own weight):

> The advantage acquired from the length of the lever is nothing but the ability to move all at once that heavy body [Bruno] which could be conducted only in pieces [of 50 pounds each] by the same force, during the same time, and with an equal motion [1 foot], without benefit of the lever.

Galileo then showed that all the other machines operated on exactly the same principle. In his analysis he reduced each of them to various forms of the lever.

Galileo reworked his treatise on mechanics several times, and numerous copies of it circulated in manuscript. It appeared in print for the first time in 1634 in French, having been published by a priest, Marin Mersenne, as *The Mechanics of Galileo, Mathematician and Engineer of the Duke of Florence.*

With his financial affairs becoming a little more stable, Galileo found time to indulge in social activities. He often visited the fabled city of Venice, with its many fine palaces along the Grand Canal, which was trafficked by singing gondoliers. There he met and fell in love with a Venetian woman, Marina Gamba. Though they never married, they had three children: Virginia, born in August 1600; Livia, born in August 1601; and Vincenzio, born in August 1606. Marina moved to Padua to raise the family, but Galileo kept her in a small house of her own, not among the student boarders in his own house.

On one of his early trips to Venice, Galileo formed an imaginative explanation for the cause of the ocean tides. Watching a barge carrying water to Venice, he noticed how the water slopped from one end of the barge to the other as the ship's speed changed. In his mind's eye he visualized the tidal flow of water in the sea as being similar to the water piling up at one end of the barge. He previously had been impressed by the size of the Venetian tidal changes, which were so much greater than those he had seen on the coast near Pisa, on the other side of Italy.

Galileo decided that ocean tides could result from the shaking of the earth. And that might be the result of the motions of the earth about its axis and around the sun—if the theory of the Polish astronomer Nicolaus Copernicus happened to be correct.

Copernicus had published his theory in 1543. He intended it to replace the model of Ptolemy that had been in use since A.D. 150. Ptolemy's model of the planets was based on Aristotle's cosmology: the earth was in the center, with the moon, sun, and five other planets circling on spheres around the earth. Copernicus, in contrast, made the earth a planet. He placed it between Venus and Mars, circling the sun with the others. Only the moon circled the earth. Both models made predictions of planetary positions with about the same accuracy. But the Ptolemaic model seemed to fit common sense better. After all, we do not feel the earth moving. *Theory of the Planets,* which Galileo taught, was based on Ptolemy's model.

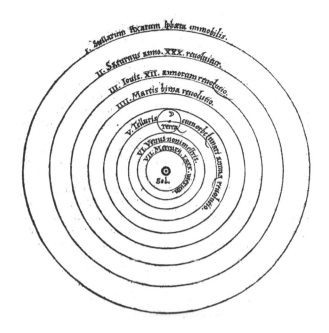

I. Stellarum fixarum sphæra immobilis.
II. Saturnus anno. XXX. reuoluitur.
III. Iouis. XII. annorum reuolutio.
IIII. Martis bima reuolutio.
V. Telluris ☽ eum orbe lunari annua reuolutio.
VI. Veneris nonimestris.
VII. Mercury LXXX.
Sol.

By placing the sun at the center of the universe, with the earth and the other planets revolving around it, Polish astronomer Nicolaus Copernicus challenged the long-held belief that the earth was the center of the universe.

Until 1595, although Galileo had been aware of the Copernican theory, he had not paid much attention to it. Now he considered that the combination of the earth's daily and yearly motions would cause regular changes in the speed of the earth in space. Perhaps that would shake the earth enough for the oceans to slop around the way the water had done in the Venetian barge. Galileo made little of this idea at the time, but in future years his theory of the tides would have grave consequences for him.

In the summer of 1602, Galileo resumed the motion studies he had abandoned while at Pisa. Until that year, the idea that objects fall with continually increasing speed had not impressed him. Now he resolved to examine various motions experimentally. We know about some of this work from a letter that Galileo wrote to Guidobaldo del Monte in November 1602. The rest comes from a careful analysis of Galileo's working papers made by Professor Stillman Drake from 1972 to 1988.

Galileo resolved to research motion by the same method astronomers had been using for 2,000 years. They

text continues on page 36

Galileo attempted to explain the tides by combining the earth's daily and annual motions. If the effect he proposed exists at all, it is very tiny. The accepted explanation for the tides relies on the gravitational attraction of the moon and the sun for the oceans differing from that for the solid earth. Such an explanation had to await Isaac Newton's work on gravity toward the end of the 1600s.

The great virtue of Galileo's idea is that it did not depend on some mysterious force reaching out from the moon to push around the oceans. He wanted his explanation to be entirely mechanical.

Here is a more detailed description of Galileo's initial idea. It is based on four paragraphs found in Paolo Sarpi's diary from 1595.

The center of the earth advances 1 degree per day in its orbit, or 30 minutes in half a day (since 1 degree = 60 minutes). Because the earth's diameter is about 6 minutes of its orbit around the sun, a point on its night side advances by 20 percent more than those 30 minutes; and a point on the day side is retarded by the same 20 percent. So, each part of the earth's surface moves now fast, now average, and then slowly, with respect to the stars.

Water carried in a moving basin remains behind at the beginning of motion and rises at the rear, because the motion has not been completely transferred to it. When the basin stops, the water continues to move and rises at the front. The seas are like waters in basins. These basins, by the combined action of the daily and annual motions of the earth, move first swiftly and then more slowly. A great sea that is more than a quarter of the earth's circumference will be partly in the earth's swifter motion, and partly in the slower.

Thus, lakes and small seas will not show tides because the speed variation in them is very small. In the larger seas, the tidal effects will differ depending on whether their length is along or across the changing motion of the earth.

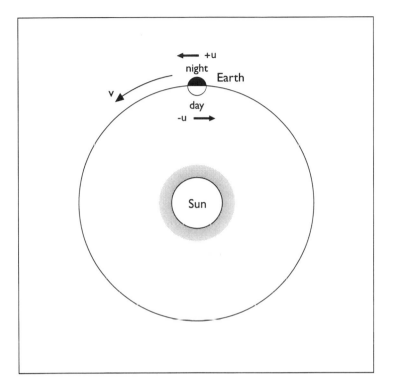

According to Galileo, the earth's daily and yearly motions combine to cause ocean tides. In the above diagram, v represents the speed of the earth in orbit around the sun; u is the speed of the earth's rotation on its axis.

The tides of the seas are composed of two parts. First, the water falls behind and rises at the rear as the earth speeds up; second, as the earth slows, the water continues forward and rises in front. Both actions are followed by the natural tendency of the water to return to equilibrium. Thus, water in a sea or ocean will oscillate back and forth at a rate that depends on the size of its basin.

invented models of the heavens, and then adjusted the models to match their observations. Galileo would create a mathematical model for the motion of objects that would produce the same numerical results for distances and times that he could measure. No one had previously taken this approach in any science except astronomy. That is why we call Galileo the "first physicist."

Although Galileo wanted to explain *vertical* fall, his experiments did not begin there. Falling occurs when a supported object has the support removed. Since falling is so quick, Galileo looked for ways to "dilute" the fall, to make it slower. He found two instances of motions that seemed to contain a *component* of free fall.

In both cases, motion started when a support was released. In the first, a ball held in a groove at the upper end of an inclined plane will roll down when released. In the second, a ball hanging on a string (a pendulum) will swing back and forth after being pulled aside and released.

Galileo's experimental measurements with inclined planes and pendulums are described on page 114. With those measurements, Galileo found several interesting and important regular numerical relationships. For a ball rolling along a gently sloping grooved board, he found that the distance traveled was proportional to the square of the time elapsed from when it started. If the ball travels 4 centimeters in 0.2 seconds, then in 0.5 seconds it travels 25 centimeters. The relation is

$$\frac{25\,cm}{4\,cm} = \frac{(0.5s)^2}{(0.2s)^2} = \frac{25}{4}$$

For pendulums, Galileo found that longer pendulums took a longer time to complete a swing than did shorter ones. He measured time by weighing water that flowed out of a narrow tube at the bottom of a bucket while the pendulum moved. Although primitive in structure, this is a quite accurate water clock. By careful measurement he showed that the time taken to complete a swing was proportional to the square root of the length of a pendulum. A one-meter pendulum swings over and back in 2 seconds. A half-meter pendulum takes 1.41 seconds ($\sqrt{2} = 1.4142$).

Galileo also used his water clock to measure several direct vertical falls. However, rather than performing a large number of such tests, he compared times of falling to the times of pendulum swings when the lengths of the pendulums were equal to the distances fallen. From the few tests he made, Galileo found a fixed numerical relation between the time of fall and the time of swing. He then established the time-squared relation very accurately for the pendulum. Secure in the accuracy of the pendulum relation, he transferred that accuracy to the times of falling.

By these results Galileo determined that distances in falling from rest increase as the square of the elapsed time. This means that the object's speed increases as it falls—the

A page of calculations from Galileo's working notes on motion.

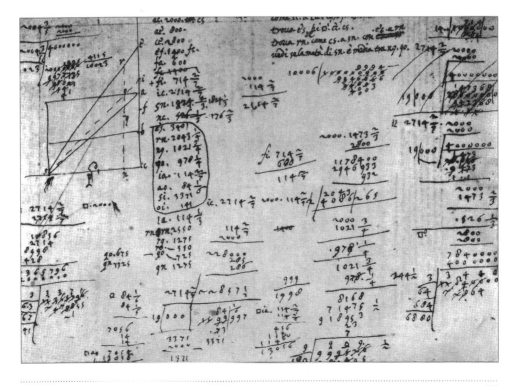

motion is accelerated. But he wanted to be able to say precisely *how* speed increases during fall, an endeavor that would take four more years of study.

Starting from a rule that speed increases with distance, Galileo deduced what that would predict for how distance increased with time. In October 1604, he wrote a letter to Paolo Sarpi that seems to claim that if speed increases in proportion to distance fallen, then distance increases with the square of the time. Although the conclusion matches experience, Galileo used flawed reasoning. By 1608, he had corrected his error. He showed that if speed increases in direct proportion to the *time*, then distance increases as the time squared. This is the same result physicists and engineers still use today.

Also in 1608, Galileo showed that the path of a projectile, such as a cannonball, follows the curve known as a parabola. With this information, he could predict the ranges of cannons, depending on the amount of gunpowder used and the angle of elevation of the cannon's barrel.

Galileo's work on motion was interrupted in October 1604. On the 15th of the month, some people noticed a new bright star in the sky. According to Aristotle, heavenly perfection did not allow *any* change—certainly not the appearance of new stars. Philosophy professors in Padua tried to argue that the new star was nearer than the moon, and therefore not in the heavens. People consulted Galileo about the new star. He received reports from many cities in Europe that made clear that the star was far beyond the moon. He determined the star's distance by using the optical principle of *parallax*. Parallax is the apparent shifting of the location of a nearby object compared to ones more distant.

When you walk along a road looking at cows in a field, their position seems to change relative to the trees beyond them. The nearer cow has a larger parallactic shift than the one farther away. In astronomy parallax can be used to find distances to planets or nearby stars. The constellations of stars take the place of the clumps of trees. And, instead of walking a little way along a road, you have to take two points far apart on the earth.

Padua is about a thousand miles from Stockholm. In Padua, the edge of the moon might be seen close to one of the stars in the constellation Pleiades. In Stockholm, the moon's edge would appear slightly shifted from that star toward one of its neighbors. From one city to the other, the moon appears to shift about 0.23 degrees relative to the background stars. That makes the distance to the moon about 250,000 miles. That is because a skinny triangle with a base of 1,000 miles and height of 250,000 miles has an apex angle of 0.23 degrees.

From the reports he received, Galileo knew that the parallactic shift of the new star was much less than that of the moon. That made it farther away than the moon. In fact, the new star showed no appreciable parallax, which definitely put it among the other stars.

This bothered the Aristotelian philosophers. They firmly believed that the heavens were perfect. No new star could appear to change the heavens. Galileo's colleague, the philosopher Cremonini, asked him to explain parallax to him because, said Cremonini, "I'm going to write against it." Which he did. Galileo made great fun of Cremonini's being opposed to something he did not understand.

Another philosopher, Ludovico delle Colombe, in Florence, wrote a book defending the perfection of the heavens. He concurred that the new star was in the heavens, but explained that it remained invisible until some kind of a lens moving in the sky revealed it to human sight.

Galileo disdainfully attacked Colombe's attempt to save Aristotle. He ridiculed the great lens in the sky that Colombe had imagined. Galileo published his attack under the pen name of Mauri. Although Colombe suspected Galileo to be the author, he could not be sure. Galileo also insulted Colombe by referring to him as *Signor Colombo,* which means "Mr. Pigeon"—whereas *delle Colombe* means "of the family of the Doves." For the rest of his life, Colombe would continue to uphold Aristotle against Galileo.

Galileo's many financial obligations always left him short of cash. The university twice renewed his teaching contract with large increases in salary. Each time, however, Galileo had to ask powerful friends to convince university authorities of his value. And he often worried that his contract would not be renewed. With the dispute over the new star of 1604, Galileo felt that his enemies might be able to get him dismissed.

It was natural, then, that Galileo began to look for other opportunities. One tactic he used was to dedicate books he wrote to prospective employers. He dedicated the book criticizing Colombe to the pope's treasurer. Galileo could inform the treasurer that he was Mauri, without letting his Venetian employers know that he was looking for a new position. In 1606, when Galileo published the handbook for his proportional compass, he dedicated it to Prince Cosimo de' Medici (aged 16), who lived in Florence.

To improve his opportunities, Galileo had already begun spending his summers in Florence tutoring young Cosimo in mathematics. Although he was not paid for anything but his living expenses, Galileo used these summers to enhance his standing with the Tuscan court.

At the invitation of the grand duchess Christina, he attended Cosimo's wedding in 1608. Then, later that year, she wrote to ask him to cast a horoscope for her ill husband, Ferdinand I. Galileo wrote back on January 16, 1609, predicting a long life. Ferdinand died 22 days later and was succeeded by Galileo's pupil, now known as Cosimo II.

Apparently the grand duchess bore Galileo no ill will for the error in his prediction. And now, with his pupil as grand duke, Galileo had more hope that he might find employment back in Florence. The opportunity came in an unexpected way.

G alileo established by measurements and calculations that the distance an object falls from a resting position increases as the square of the elapsed time. But he wanted to be able to describe how speed increases during a fall. Since he could not measure speed, he tried to devise a theory for the increase in speed. For some time, however, he was unsure whether to say that speed increased uniformly with distance or with time.

Galileo's problem was to find a rule for the way an object's speed increased as it fell. Since he could not measure speeds directly, he had to arrive at their measurements by mathematical deduction. He started by assuming a rule for speeds and then calculated what distances his rule would produce. He could then check calculated distances against measured ones.

For a while, Galileo seemed to have thought that the increase in speed was proportional to the distance fallen. That is not correct. Later, he tried a new rule—that speed increased in proportion to elapsed time. If that is correct, then how could he find the distances that rule produced?

Consider the graph below. It represents an object traveling at a constant speed of 7 meters per second for 4 seconds. The distance traveled is

$$7\frac{m}{s} \times 4s = 28m$$

You get distance by multiplying the values of speed and time. When those values are represented by the height and breadth of a rectangle, their product gives the area of the rectangle. We may say that area on a speed–time graph represents distance.

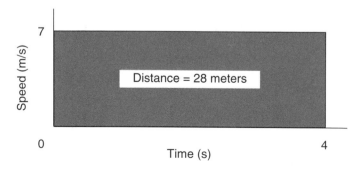

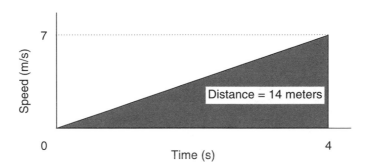

The graph above represents an object increasing its speed uniformly from 0 to 7 meters per second in 4 seconds. If the shaded area represents the distance traveled, it is 14 meters—just half the distance in the previous graph.

With algebra, we can write v for speed, t for time, and d for distance. Then,

1. $v = kt$

2. $d = \dfrac{1}{2}vt$

3. $d = \dfrac{1}{2}kt^2$

where k is the value by which you have to multiply the time to get the speed. In our example, that number would be 7/4 m/s². For fall near the earth's surface, k is the acceleration of gravity, $g = 9.8$ m/s².

The result in equation (3) of combining equations (1) and (2) shows that the distance increases in proportion to the square of the time. And that is the result Galileo found in his experimental measurements. The graphs shown here are based on the description of accelerated motion Galileo gave in his book *Two New Sciences* (1638).

SIDEREVS,
NVNCIVS
MAGNA, LONGEQVE ADMIRA-
bilia Spectacula pandens, suspiciendaq; pro-
ponens vnicuiq;, præsertim vero

PHILOSOPHIS, atq; ASTRONOMIS, quæ

GALILEO GALILEO PA-
TRITIO FLORENTINO
Patauini Gymnasii Publico
Mathematico
PERSPICILLI
Nuper a se reperti beneficio sunt obseruata in LVNÆ FA-
CIE, FIXIS INNVMERIS, LACTEO CIRCVLO
STELLIS NEBVLOSIS,
Apprime vero in
QVATVOR PLANETIS
Circa IOVIS Stellam disparibus interuallis, atq; periodis,
celeritate mirabili circumuolutis; quos, nemini in hanc vsq;
diem cognitos, nouissime Auctor depre-
hendit primus; atque
MEDICEA SIDERA
NVNCVPANDOS DECREVIT.

M. D   C. X

Prostat Francof. in Paltheniano.

Galileo's Starry Messenger (Siderius Nuncius), was so popular that all 550 copies of the first edition, which was printed in Venice in 1610, were sold within a week. A reprint (shown here) in Frankfurt the same year helped to fill the continuing demand.

New Wonders in the Sky

In March 1610, European scholars buzzed with excitement over a recently published booklet. In his *Starry Messenger,* Galileo reported sights in the sky never before seen. Three in particular stood out. The moon is not a smoothly polished orb. Rather it is rough and uneven, with mountains, valleys, and craters. They cannot be seen by the unaided eye, but Galileo had produced a telescope that could magnify them 20 times.

The telescope also revealed many more stars than anyone had ever imagined. Just in the region of the belt and sword of the constellation Orion, Galileo marked 80 stars. By eye alone one could make out only three stars in the belt and six in the sword. Wherever he turned his telescope, Galileo saw ten times as many stars as had been known before. The telescope also showed the Milky Way to be not just a hazy patch, but clusters of myriads of stars. Most astonishing of all, Galileo reported that four tiny moons circled Jupiter.

Galileo's surprising announcements prompted strong support from some astronomers and vehement objections from others. Several of them soon published pamphlets on the new discoveries, some for and some against. A major difficulty was that hardly anyone else had a telescope as good as Galileo's. Astronomers who soon got better instruments generally confirmed his observations.

What events had led to Galileo's astounding discoveries? How had he achieved so much in less than eight months? In the summer of 1609, Galileo heard of a new invention. Spectacle makers in Holland had recently made spyglasses that magnified distant objects three or four times. About a foot long, they had a convex lens at one end and a concave lens for the eyepiece at the other end. Peddlers were offering such telescopes for sale on the streets of Paris.

Paolo Sarpi in Venice wrote Galileo that an enterprising foreigner had offered to sell the secret of the spyglass to the government there. Sarpi was confident that Galileo could find the secret and improve on it. Knowing that the spyglass had two lenses, Galileo decided he could make a better instrument. Early in August he began to try out pairs of lenses that focused light to spots at different distances, or focal lengths.

Galileo started with spectacle lenses and found the secret of the two kinds of lenses. He and his artisan Mazzoleni then began to grind special lenses. They made the convex

text continues on page 48

A lens-grinding lathe used in Florence in the 1620s.

OPTICS AND TELESCOPES

Lenses are curved pieces of glass that change the direction of light. When you look through a lens at an object, the image may appear larger or smaller than the object. It depends on the kind of lens and the distance of the object from the lens.

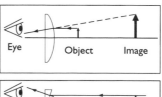

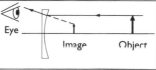

Lenses were first used for eyeglasses in Italy a few years before 1300. At first they helped people who could not focus nearby objects clearly. These include farsighted people and others whose eyes' own lenses lose flexibility with age. Lenses for them are convex, thicker in the center than at the edges.

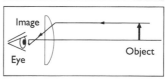

Nearsighted people cannot focus distant objects. Their vision can be improved by using concave lenses. The lens brings distant objects to a focus on the person's retina. Images seen through concave lenses are always smaller than the objects. Concave lenses began to be made and used around 1450.

If you look at a distant object through a convex lens the image appears smaller and inverted. Shortly after 1600, a Dutch lens maker combined convex and concave lenses to make distant objects appear closer (and larger).

Galileo improved the original Dutch design by using a thinner convex objective lens—a longer focal length of about 4 feet. He also used a much stronger (shorter focal length) concave eyepiece. Both changes increase magnification. He made his discoveries with a telescope of about 20 power. Telescopes of this type have a practical limit of about 30 power.

Later telescopes used convex eyepieces with longer focal length objective lenses. They could produce much greater magnifications. Christiaan Huygens made some telescopes that were well over 100 feet long.

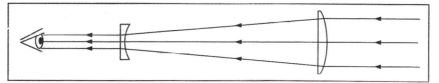

text continued from page 46

objective lens weaker, that is, less curved, with a longer focal length. And they made the concave eyepiece stronger (with a shorter focal length) by grinding it more deeply. In a couple of days they had a magnification greater than four times. Galileo wrote to tell Sarpi of his success. Sarpi advised the government to save its money and reject the foreigner's offer—the government officials took his advice.

Galileo then worked to produce a really superior spyglass. We will call it a telescope even though that name was not actually invented until 1611. When Galileo had achieved a magnifying power of about nine times, he took his new telescope to Venice. There, he demonstrated it to members of the Venetian senate. He wrote to his brother-in-law in Florence about the event: "Many of the nobles and senators, although of great age, mounted more than once to the top of the highest church tower in Venice, in order to see sails and shipping that were so far off that it was two hours before they were seen, without my spyglass, steering full sail into the harbor."

Galileo made a gift of his improved telescope to the governors of Venice. In return, they gave him a lifetime contract at the University of Padua. They also increased his salary to 1,000 florins. During this time, Galileo had been seeking employment with the grand duke in Florence. Rather than continuing to teach in Padua, he preferred to spend all his time in research and writing. But the Venetian

Two of Galileo's early telescopes, between 4 and 5 feet long.

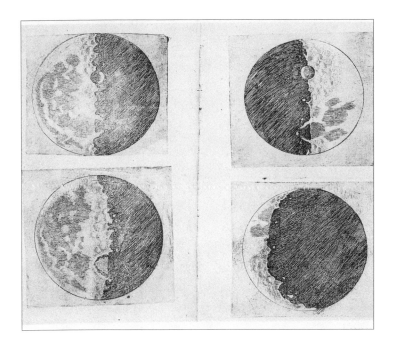

With the powerful new telescope he perfected in November 1609, Galileo was able to see and draw the surface of the moon with remarkable clarity.

offer seemed too good to refuse. Nonetheless, Galileo made a hurried trip to Florence in October. He wanted to explain why the telescope had been given to the Venetians and not to his own people in Florence. He presented a fine telescope to Grand Duke Cosimo II de' Medici and returned to Padua, confident that he had succeeded in making amends.

As the year drew to a close, Galileo continued to grind lenses. Soon he had perfected a telescope with a magnifying power of 20. He had previously shown the moon to the grand duke through a less powerful telescope. At the end of November 1609, Galileo pointed his new telescope at the moon and was amazed at the clarity of the rough features on the moon's surface. For the next month he made frequent observations of the moon. He sketched the main features as the moon went from first quarter through full to last quarter—a complete cycle of the moon's phases.

Galileo concentrated on the boundary between the lighted and dark parts of the crescent moon. He saw that the boundary was uneven. That situation came from many small dark spots just inside the lighted part. And there were small bright spots in the dark part. As time passed, the dark spots gradually became lighted. And new bright spots appeared farther into the moon's body.

Galileo reasoned that these observations matched conditions on earth. Consider chains of mountains. As the sun rises, peaks on the western chain shine brightly, while valleys east of them are dark. The valleys are shaded by mountains still farther to the east. Soon, Galileo used surveying geometry to calculate that some mountains on the moon were as high as four miles.

Then, on January 7, 1610, Galileo made a startling observation. Near Jupiter he saw three tiny starlets aligned with Jupiter's equator, two to the east and one to the west. He observed Jupiter carefully for the next few nights. Since Jupiter moves against the background of the stars, Galileo expected it to leave the starlets behind. But, by January 15, his observations made clear to him that something else was happening.

The starlets kept up with Jupiter, and different numbers of them appeared on one side or the other. On January 13, Galileo saw four starlets for the first time. Three were on the west and one on the east. Galileo now became convinced that these were not stars, but the moons of Jupiter. They circled Jupiter the way our moon circles the earth— or, as he said, the way Venus and Mercury circle the sun.

Here, for the first time, Galileo had new evidence that might support the Copernican system. Jupiter is a planet, and Jupiter has moons. Since the earth has a moon, maybe the earth is a planet circling the sun. While the logic is not compelling, it is suggestive. Up to this time, Aristotelians had argued that the earth was the center of the universe because everything seemed to revolve around it, and no other object was the center of any rotations. Now, with moons in orbit around Jupiter, that argument was clearly invalid.

Every evening Galileo recorded the positions of Jupiter's moons. Occasionally he observed until midnight or later. Soon he began to write a report of his discoveries for immediate publication. In mid-March 1610, 550 copies of his *Starry Messenger* were ready to be sent out from the press in Venice.

Galileo wrote his 60-page booklet in Latin in order to make his results accessible to scholars all across Europe. He dedicated the work to the grand duke, his former pupil in Florence. He also named Jupiter's moons the Medicean stars in honor of Grand Duke Cosimo de' Medici and his three brothers. Galileo immediately sent a special copy of the *Starry Messenger* to the grand duke, along with the telescope he used to make the discoveries. That way, Cosimo could confirm the observations for himself.

During the Easter holidays in early April, Galileo hurried to Florence. There he cemented relations with the grand duke. He also began to negotiate in earnest for a post in Cosimo's retinue, though he must have known that would make the Venetian officials unhappy.

But Galileo longed for his native land. He had also discovered that his salary increase at Padua would not begin until the fall of 1610. Even worse, the salary was fixed, never again to be increased. Galileo decided he did not want to be condemned to teaching for the rest of his life.

Late in April, Galileo returned to Padua by way of Bologna. Astronomers there had great doubts about the existence of Jupiter's moons. Galileo demonstrated his telescope, but the Bolognans seemed unable to see those moons. One of them wrote a scathing pamphlet challenging Galileo's discoveries.

Back in Padua, Galileo received a letter from Johannes Kepler, Europe's leading astronomer, who was employed at the court of the Holy Roman Emperor in Prague. Kepler encouraged Galileo by supporting the new discoveries. Through the summer and fall of 1610, Galileo made nearly 100 telescopes. Only about 1 in 10 was good enough to reveal

Jupiter's moons. Galileo sent these instruments to various European rulers to give them a chance to confirm his observations.

Galileo soon completed negotiations to return to Florence. At the end of May 1610 he was appointed chief mathematician, without teaching duties, at the University of Pisa. In addition, he was named Philosopher and First Mathematician to the Grand Duke of Tuscany. His salary was the same as the Venetians had offered. In addition, Galileo was absolved from having to make any further payments for the dowries of his two sisters.

Galileo moved to Florence in September, taking his two daughters with him. They would be cared for by his mother and sisters. His son remained with Marina Gamba for a few years and then moved to Florence. Soon after, Marina married a Paduan employed by a wealthy family.

Girls and women were not always well treated in those days. Because they were illegitimate, Galileo's daughters had no prospects for marriage, and he seemed unwilling to be responsible for their daily care. So, Galileo sought to have them admitted to a convent. To do that he had to get a friendly cardinal to waive the rule that young women were not allowed to enter the convent until they were 16. And Galileo had to pay a modest dowry and regular fees for their room and board.

The two girls were admitted to the Convent of San Matteo in October 1613. The convent was located in Arcetri, a hilltop village just south of Florence.

German astronomer Johannes Kepler corresponded with Galileo and encouraged his observations.

In the convent they engaged in gardening, cooking, and embroidery—the "feminine" pursuits of that age. And when each girl reached 16, she joined the Sisters of St. Francis.

During his first winter back in Florence, Galileo's health suffered. He had frequent bouts of the fever and rheumatism that plagued him for the rest of his life. From time to time Galileo could get some relief by staying with his friend Filippo Salviati, a young nobleman interested in literature and science. Salviati owned a fine country estate called Le Selve, a few miles west of Florence. While at Salviati's villa, Galileo rested, wrote, and discussed science with his host's other friends. Unfortunately, Salviati died in 1614 at the early age of 32.

Initial opposition to Galileo's discoveries came from conservative astronomers and philosophers. At first, they claimed that the new objects were not in the sky but in the telescope. But soon, enough people had seen the new wonders for themselves for this objection to subside.

Some philosophers simply refused to look. Galileo's Paduan colleague Cremonini was writing a book about Aristotle's astronomical views. He neglected Galileo's discoveries because he said he had not seen them. But he would not look because he said spectacles gave him a headache. The pain might have been as much in his philosophy as in his head.

Kepler in Prague finally managed to borrow a telescope. He observed Jupiter's moons for several months. Then he published a booklet that fully supported Galileo's observations. But others objected to Galileo's interpretations, especially that the moon had a rough surface. Philosophers who followed Aristotle were convinced that the moon, a heavenly object, had to be perfectly smooth. Several of them tried to defend that notion. One was Ludovico delle Colombe, the staunch Aristotelian who had imagined a celestial lens to explain the new star of 1604.

Galileo included these sketches of Saturn in a letter to a friend in 1612.

Now he directed his fertile imagination to the purity of the moon. Colombe proposed that although the moon's dark surface might be rough, it was enclosed by an invisible crystal substance with a perfectly smooth surface.

Galileo replied with ridicule: "If Colombe wishes to imagine the moon surrounded by transparent invisible crystal, I will grant that, if he allows me to say that its surface is covered with gigantic mountains, equally invisible. Such pretty fictions are worthless, since they can never be proved."

When he was able to work, Galileo had two main occupations. The first was using his telescope to examine other planets, especially Venus. He also observed Saturn with its rings, although his telescope lacked the power to show the rings clearly. Because of this Galileo often drew the planet so it looked like it had ears. He spoke of these as companions of Saturn, and he said they did not orbit Saturn as Jupiter's moons orbited it.

Galileo did not observe Venus until the autumn of 1610. The previous winter it had been the morning star, and we may suppose that Galileo usually slept until after dawn. In October, Venus—as evening star—shone brightly in the western sky for an hour or so after dusk. Initially, Galileo saw Venus as a small round globe. Later, it appeared to wane gradually, showing phases like the moon's. In mid-December Venus was just half-illuminated, and still waning.

At the end of December 1610, Venus showed a distinct crescent shape, with the horns pointing away from the sun. Galileo wrote several letters to announce this new discovery. To his colleague Benedetto Castelli he wrote:

I began to observe Venus about three months ago. I saw it round in shape and very small. Daily it grew in bulk and kept round, until when it was very distant [in angle] from the Sun, it began to lose its roundness on the eastern side [opposite the Sun], and in a few days was a half-circle. It stayed that shape for many days, but always growing in size. Now it begins to become sickle-shaped; as long as it is seen in the evening it will go on thinning its little horns until they vanish.

As Venus began showing the crescent shape, its apparent diameter increased. Galileo realized this meant that Venus was getting closer to earth. When Venus was small and almost round, it was farther away than the sun; when larger and crescent-shaped, it was nearer than the sun. These observations convinced Galileo that Venus orbited the sun, as described in the Copernican scheme. For the first time he felt he had strong visual evidence to support Copernicus.

Galileo's other occupation was to make precise calculations of the periods of the moons of Jupiter. He found it hard to tell the four little moons apart. He did see that an inner moon seemed to move from one side of Jupiter to the other in about a day. This suggested that it might take about 48 hours to complete its orbit.

He also saw that another moon moved much farther out than the others. It seemed to take about half a month to complete an orbit. Kepler, who was observing Jupiter's

Galileo's values for the periods of Jupiter's moons are quite close to modern values.

Jupiter's moons	I (Io)	II (Europa)	III (Ganymede)	IV (Callisto)
Galileo, 1612	1 d, 18 h, 26 m	3 d, 13 h, 22 m	7 d, 3 h, 26 m	16 d, 12 h, 21 m
Galileo, 1617	1 d, 18 h, 28.6 m	3 d, 13 h, 17.7 m	7 d, 3 h, 58.2 m	16 d, 17 h, 58.7 m
Modern values	1 d, 18 h, 28.6 m	3 d, 13 h, 17.9 m	7 d, 3 h, 59.6 m	16 d, 18 h, 5.1 m

moons at the same time as Galileo, despaired of ever getting the orbital periods of all four. But Galileo persisted.

He made frequent observations. He recorded times, positions, and brightnesses. As a good scientist does, he collected all the available data. He realized that when he got a model he could test, these data would be invaluable. Then, one evening in mid-March 1611, Galileo was unable to see any of Jupiter's moons. Perhaps some were behind Jupiter, and some directly in front. Galileo took this moment as a starting point for all four motions. As the moons became visible, he tracked them. He began to measure and calculate their speeds of motion.

By early 1612, with many revisions, Galileo had calculated the moons' periods. Five years later, he had refined them even further. The table on page 55 shows how close Galileo came to the modern values. Galileo now felt that his work would benefit from support by the Jesuits. These members of the Society of Jesus were among the leading scientists of Europe. Their chief training center was the Roman College. The dean of the mathematicians at the Roman College was Christoph Clavius. Galileo knew that his agreement would be crucial in establishing these new discoveries.

When Galileo's health improved in the spring of 1611, he resolved to visit Rome. The grand duke provided him with a carriage. During the six-day journey, Galileo made nightly observations of Jupiter's moons at stops along the way. He arrived in Rome on March 29, 1611.

Before Galileo arrived, Clavius had obtained a good telescope. With it, he and his fellow Jesuits had confirmed all of Galileo's observations. Although Clavius agreed with the observations, he differed from Galileo in his interpretations. In particular, Clavius was still closely bound to Aristotle's ideas. He could not accept the roughness of the moon. Instead, Clavius considered the moon's smooth surface to consist of regions of varying density. Apparently

Galileo's argument about the changing bright and dark spots did not convince Clavius. Other Jesuit mathematicians, however, did agree that the moon had a rough surface.

While in Rome, Galileo received a boost of support from an unexpected quarter. Eight years earlier, a wealthy young nobleman in Rome had begun a scientific society. Not yet 20 at the time, Prince Federigo Cesi founded the Lincean Academy with a few friends. This society was named for the lynx, an animal esteemed for its keen sight. The young men decided to devote their time (and money) to expanding their knowledge of the world.

On April 14, 1611, Prince Cesi invited Galileo to a banquet. He wanted the scientist to demonstrate the telescope to his other guests. It was at this meeting that the group invented the name *telescopium* for Galileo's new instrument. This Latin word was coined from the Greek root words *tele* (far off) and *scopein* (to look)—an instrument for looking far off. The new word soon became naturalized into English as *telescope,* and in Italian as *telescopio.*

Soon after, Cesi invited Galileo to join the Linceans. Galileo was delighted by the chance to share his ideas with others of like mind. His membership also greatly enhanced the Academy's reputation. Within about a year its roster increased from 4 to 20 members. Galileo also helped Cesi to set the agenda for the academy's activities.

The Lincean Academy sponsored the publication of two of Galileo's next books. In addi-

The crest of the Lincean Academy, founded in 1603 by Prince Federigo Cesi and a few friends. Members devoted themselves to expanding their knowledge of the world. Galileo joined the academy in 1611.

tion to holding meetings and publishing books, members of the academy carried on a lively correspondence. About 100 letters per year from 1611 to 1615 survive in the Academy's correspondence files. With these letters, the Linceans kept one another informed about their ideas and discoveries. The activities of the Lincean Academy demonstrate how important communication is in the development of science. Unfortunately, the Academy declined at the time of Cesi's early death in 1630.

While in Rome, Galileo began to think more intently about the Copernican arrangement of the planets. His telescopic discoveries had convinced him that Aristotle had been seriously in error. But he felt that Ptolemy's scheme was little better. Both ancient theories placed the earth in the center of the universe, with the sun, moon, and other planets orbiting about it. Galileo's observations showed Venus to be orbiting the sun. Both Jupiter and earth had moons. None of the planets, nor the earth, produced light of their own. They all shone by reflecting light from the sun.

In fact, in his *Starry Messenger,* Galileo had correctly explained the faint light that illuminates the body of the moon early in its first quarter. It comes from earthshine—sunlight reflected from the earth to the moon. At such times, the daylight side of the earth faces the moon. So Galileo claimed that the moon is earthlike, and that the earth is planetlike. And that the earth and the planets orbit the sun . . . so the earth is a planet.

Galileo then began to promote the system of Copernicus, which put the earth into orbit around the sun. This action aroused strong opposition from Aristotelian philosophers. They looked for ways to explain away Galileo's observations. And they demanded that he prove the earth's motion.

Galileo could not satisfy their demands for such proof. In his approach to science, he worked by building up evidence piece by piece. By now, he felt that the evidence leaned toward Copernicus. As the years went by, Galileo constructed various arguments to show that having the earth move was at least as reasonable as having it at rest. Before long, the philosophers who opposed Galileo would seek assistance from theologians. If they could not disprove Galileo's ideas, they would charge him with contradicting the Bible.

In the meantime, Galileo's two-month visit to Rome was a complete triumph. A Florentine cardinal reported to Cosimo II:

> During his stay here, Galileo has given great satisfaction. He showed his discoveries so well that all learned men found them as true and well-founded as they were aston-ishing. If we still followed ancient Roman traditions, I truly believe they would have erected a column to cele-brate him.

Pope Paul V honored Galileo by granting him an audience. The pope showed great good will for the mathematician of the grand duke of Tuscany. A number of church and civic leaders gave banquets for him. And the Jesuits of the Roman College held a meeting for him in which they praised and supported his discoveries.

Galileo returned to Florence at the end of May 1611, greatly heartened by his Roman success. However, he soon became embroiled in a dispute with philosophers in Florence over an entirely different matter. These philoso-phers opposed him relentlessly.

GALILAEUS GALILAEI PATRICIUS FLÖR.
AET. SUAE
ANNUM AGENS QUADRAGESIMUM.

Sanctes Titi pinxit   *Ex Pinacotheca A diana*   *Joseph Calendi sculp.*
Raph Morghen direxit

This, the earliest known portrait of Galileo, was done around 1603, when he was 39.

Disputes in Philosophy and Science

The banquet hall glittered. Grand Duke Cosimo, with his wife, mother, and brothers, watched proudly as the servants presented the feast. Two cardinals, princes of the Church, were the guests of honor. For entertainment, two members of Cosimo's retinue would engage in a philosophical dispute.

Galileo, philosopher and chief mathematician to the grand duke, was the star attraction. Professor Flaminio Papazzoni, a philosopher at the University of Pisa, defended Aristotle against Galileo's attacks. The professor claimed that broad shapes floated on water and that narrow ones sank.

To the delight of the court, Galileo demonstrated the opposite. He had small cones of wax weighted with lead filings so that they were slightly more dense than water. They floated when placed on water with their sharp ends down and sank when put the other way round. You could demonstrate this with the chocolate chips used for making cookies.

The dispute had begun innocently enough. In July 1611, Salviati had entertained Galileo and some philosophers at his palace in Florence. During the evening, their talk turned to Aristotle's views on the states of matter.

Galileo wrote an account of this conversation soon afterward:

> One of the philosophers said that the action of cold is to condense; and he claimed that ice is nothing but condensed water.
>
> I questioned that, saying that we should rather call ice rarefied water. That is because condensing makes things heavier; and since ice floats on water, it must be lighter.
>
> "No," said the philosopher, "ice does not float because it is lighter than water, but because it is broad and flat." I had two answers to that. "First," I said, "any shape of ice will float, not just broad, thin sheets." And I added, "Would you expect that if ice is denser than water, then if you pushed it under the surface, it would easily return to float at the surface?" To that he had no reply.

The philosopher then said that if you strike water with the flat side of a sword, you feel a great resistance, whereas if you strike with the edge, the sword penetrates easily. Galileo replied that an object's shape affects the speed of its motion through water, but not whether something will sink or float. He concluded, "If a given material will sink when it is in the shape of a sphere, then it will also sink if it has any other shape."

The philosophers were doubly angry. Not only had Galileo contradicted their idea about floating, he had also challenged their understanding of Aristotle. The dispute soon became public. An old opponent of Galileo's entered the fray. Ludovico delle Colombe claimed he could demonstrate the effect of shape on floating. Ebony, a type of wood, is slightly more dense than water. That could be shown by the sinking of an ebony ball in water. But a flat chip of ebony floated when placed on the surface of water. Colombe challenged Galileo to debate him in public.

At this point Grand Duke Cosimo intervened. He ordered Galileo not to make a spectacle of himself. Cosimo felt the dispute would be too much like brawling in the streets. Obediently, Galileo wrote an account of the events for Cosimo. He said he would also write a book to explain all kinds of floating. But, he added, he would welcome a chance to debate the issues at the Tuscan court—with a discreet regard for decorum. He would demonstrate his worth as the grand duke's philosopher.

The banquet for the cardinals was held on October 2, 1611. Galileo won the support of the senior visiting cardinal, Maffeo Barberini, who came from a noble Florentine family. He developed a liking for Galileo, which continued after he became Pope Urban VIII in 1623.

However, the other cardinal, son of the duke of Mantua, took the Aristotelian side. Though the court was greatly entertained by the philosophical dispute, no clear winner emerged. Both sides considered themselves vindicated by the interest shown in them by such eminent officials.

Soon after the banquet, Galileo was taken ill, and he retired to Salviati's villa. His recurring fever forced him to bed, but the country air at Salviati's villa helped him to endure his pains. He spent the winter there writing his book on floating bodies. In the book, Galileo claimed that Archimedes had explained all kinds of floating. A body less dense than water floats because the water can support a weight equal to the weight of water in the space the body occupies.

But how to explain the floating of the little cones more dense than water? Galileo examined the situation closely. He saw that the cones sat in a small depression in the water. We now say that water molecules exert a sideways force at their surface—we call it surface tension. But Galileo did not know about that. He did know that the depression had a limit of about one-eighth of an inch.

He treated the "wall" of the depression as part of the cone. Thus, he said, the cone has the air in the depression "attached" to it. Since the combination of cone and air is

text continues on page 65

FLOATING ON THE SURFACE OF WATER

A ccording to Archimedes' principle of flotation, water exerts an upward thrust on an object immersed in it. The upward force is equal to the weight of the water the object displaces. An object less dense than water submerges only until it displaces an amount of water equal to its own weight. An object of the same density as water will float with its upper surface level with the water's surface.

Galileo's opponents claimed that small chips denser than water floated because of their broad shape. Galileo rejected the idea that shape had anything to do with it. He claimed that Archimedes principle of flotation still applied. All that mattered was the relative density of the object compared to water.

To illustrate this, Galileo performed several experiments, which he explained as follows (the numbers match the diagrams from top to bottom):

1. A small chip of ebony (denser than water) can be placed gently at the surface of water. It will descend a bit into the water and float there if it is not wetted. There is a tiny wall of water above the chip in the depression.

2. According to Galileo, the air within the depression is "attached" to the chip. The combination of air and chip has the same volume as the water displaced. The chip (plus air) floats because its average density equals the density of water.

3. An inverted cone floats for the same reason as the chip. The "attached" air in the space above the flat base reduces the density of the floating cone.

4. When the cone is placed on the water with its base down, the wall of water closes in on the sloping sides of the cone.

5. The space around the point is too small to allow enough air to be "attached" to reduce the density of the cone so that it will float. Therefore, the cone sinks when placed base down on the water.

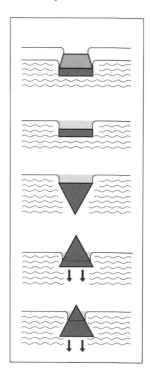

text continued from page 63

less dense than water, it floats, following Archimedes' principle of floating bodies. Galileo said it was not different from having an iron pot float on water. The iron is much more dense than water, but the iron plus the contained air is less dense than water.

What about the paradox of the cone? Having the point down allows a substantial volume of air in the depression above it. But with the point up, the depression closes in on the cone, without space for enough air to attach to the cone. Galileo also saw clearly that the walls of the depression would collapse if the top of the floating object got wet. Then it would sink immediately to the bottom, just like an iron pot that had been filled with water.

Galileo called his book *Discourse on bodies that stay atop water or move within it*, which is often shortened to *Bodies in Water*. It contained all the arguments and experiments he had used about floating. It also contained a good description of the logic involved in Archimedes' principle of floating. Where appropriate Galileo provided calculations and mathematical theorems.

Bodies in Water was published in the spring of 1612. Galileo wrote it in Italian, as he did almost all of his later books. In those days, it was much more common to write such books in Latin. But Galileo said he wanted to encourage young men who did not have a chance to go to college. He wanted them to read his books and realize they were intelligent enough to understand new ideas.

Philosophers in Florence and Pisa were greatly annoyed by the favor Galileo was gaining with the grand duke. Four of them wrote short books attacking *Bodies in Water*. In Florence, they formed a group around Ludovico delle Colombe to find ways to discredit Galileo. Galileo and his friends made fun of them, calling them the Pigeon League, again punning on Colombe's name.

In the spring of 1612 Galileo returned to Florence in improved health. Awaiting him were letters that had not

Difcorfo di

le cagioni però affegnate cosí fon difettofe, ne è vero che'l folido, nel fommergerfi, follevi, e fcacci mole d'acqua eguale alla fua propria fommerfa: anzi l'acqua follevata è fempre meno, che la parte del folido ch'è fommerfa: e tanto più, quanto il vafo, nel quale fi contien l'acqua, è più ftretto: di modo che non repugna che vn folido poffa fommergerfi tutto fott'acqua fenza pure alzarne tanta, che, in mole, pareggi la decima, o la ventefima parte della fua mole: sì come all'incontro piccolifsima quantità d'acqua potrà follevare vna grandifsima mole folida, ancorchè tal folido pefaffe affolutamente cento è più volte di effa acqua, tutta volta che la materia di tal folido fia in ifpecie men graue dell'acqua: e così vna grandifsima traue, che v g. pefi 1000. libbre, potrà effere alzata, e foftenuta da acqua, che non ne pefi 50: e quefto auuerrà, quando il momento dell'acqua venga compenfato dalla velocità del fuo moto. Ma perchè tali cofe, profferite così in aftratto, hanno qualche difficultà all'effer comprefe, è bene che vegniamo à dimoftrarle con efempli particolari; e per ageuolezza della dimoftrazione intenderemo i vafi, ne' quali s'abbia ad infonder l'acqua, e fituare i folidi, effer circondati, e racchiufi da fponde erette à perpendicolo fopra'l piano dell'orizzonte, e'l folido da porfi in tali vafi effere ò cilindro retto, ò prifma pur retto. E prima dimoftrerremo, che quando in vno de' vafi fopraddetti, di qualunq; larghezza, benchè immenfa, ò angufta, fia collocato vn tal prifma, ò cilindro, circondato da acqua, fe alzeremo tal folido à perpendicolo, l'acqua circunfufa s'abbafferà, e l'abbaffamento dell'acqua all'alzamento del prifma aurà la medefima proporzione, che l'vna delle bafe del prifma, alla fuperficie dell'acqua circunfufa.

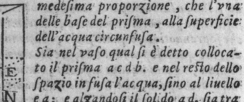

Sia nel vafo qual fi è detto collocato il prifma a c d b. e nel refto dello fpazio infufa l'acqua, fino al liuello e a: e alzandofi il folido a d. fia trasferito in g m. e l'acqua s'abbafsi da e a. in n o. Dico che la fcefa dell'acqua mifurata dalla linea a o. alla falita del prifma, mifurata dalla linea g a. hà la fteffa proporzione, che la bafe del folido g h. alla fuperficie dell'acqua n o. Il che è manifefto: perchè la mole del folido g a b h. alzata fopra'l liuello e a b. è eguale alla mole dell'acqua, che fi è abbaffata e n o a.

Son

A page from Bodies in Water. *By writing in Italian, rather than Latin, as was customary for most scholars of the time, Galileo hoped to reach a broad audience.*

been sent on to him at Le Selve. One in particular was of special interest.

It came from Mark Welser, a civic official in southern Germany, much interested in science. Welser sought Galileo's comments about a pamphlet he enclosed. It was written by a Jesuit mathematician from a nearby college who wished to remain anonymous. Later, Galileo learned that his name was Christoph Scheiner. Scheiner wrote that his telescope had revealed dark spots in front of the sun.

These sunspots provided grave difficulties for Aristotelians, who considered the sun to be an immaculate body. Scheiner proposed that the spots were not actually on the sun's surface. Instead, he suggested that clusters of many little stars circulated around the sun and became visible when they passed in front of the sun's face.

Galileo had already seen sunspots for himself. He had shown them to people in Rome a year earlier. At the time, he had not paid much attention to them. After reading Scheiner's pamphlet, he began to observe the sunspots regularly.

Immediately, Galileo realized two things. First, the breadth of each sunspot seemed to change from day to day as it moved across the face of the sun. The change in shape was exactly what you would expect if the spots were on the sun's spherical surface. That is, they were narrower when seen at the sun's edge than when they were nearer the middle. It was like looking at a disk tilted away from you, instead of seeing it full face.

Second, Galileo realized that the sun must be rotating on its axis. He soon estimated that its rate of rotation is about once a month. He did this by following the course of a single spot for more than a month. Although the spots come in varying shapes and sizes, sometimes a spot is large enough to persist longer than the time the sun takes to make a complete rotation. So, after vanishing at the western edge, it reappears at the eastern edge two weeks

*Galileo's detailed obser-
vations of sunspots led
him to conclude that the
sun rotates on its axis in
less than a month.*

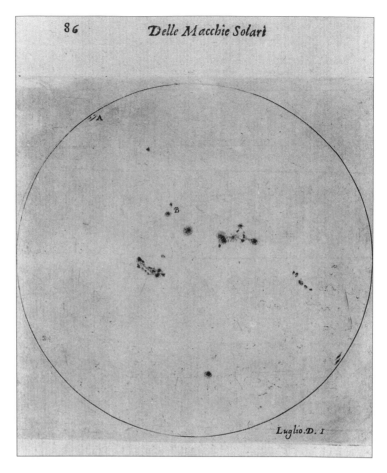

later. This allowed Galileo to measure the time of solar rotation.

Galileo soon had ample information to reply to Welser's questions. In a long letter, he described his observations and then considered what the spots might be like. He compared them to stars and to clouds. Going over them feature by feature, he showed that the sunspots resembled clouds much more than stars. But Galileo did not say positively that the spots were clouds. He wrote:

> I do not assert that the spots are clouds of the same material as ours, or watery vapors raised from the earth and attracted by the sun. I merely say that we know nothing that resembles them more closely. They may be vapors or exhala-

tions, or clouds, or fumes sent out from the sun's globe, or attracted there from other places. I do not decide on this— they may be any other of a thousand things we cannot conceive.

Galileo also took the opportunity to describe a clever technique for recording sunspots that was devised by his friend Benedetto Castelli. Castelli fastened a sheet of paper to a frame less than a meter from the eyepiece lens. Pointed at the sun, the telescope would form an image of the sun on the paper. The frame could be adjusted so that a circle drawn on the paper could just enclose the sun's image. Then he outlined the spots as they appeared on the paper. This method was a godsend for allowing observers to avoid looking directly at the sun.

In all, Galileo wrote three letters to Welser about sunspots. The third was a reply to a second pamphlet that Scheiner published to answer Galileo's first two letters. Copies of Galileo's letters were sent to Cesi in Rome, who decided to have them printed by the Lincean Academy. Written in Italian, they appeared in the spring of 1613 with the title *History and Demonstrations concerning Sunspots and Their Phenomena*. This book is commonly called *Letters on Sunspots*.

In addition to Galileo's letters, the book included predictions of the locations of Jupiter's moons for the following three months. This showed that Galileo had made great headway in determining the motions of those little moons. Observers of the moons could compare their observations with his predictions to see how accurate he had been.

With his *Letters on Sunspots* published, Galileo turned to other tasks. Two in particular occupied his time: using Jupiter's moons to determine the longitude of any location on earth, and noting objections to his *Bodies in Water* published by his four opponents.

Galileo knew that longitude could be found if you knew the time absolutely—not just relative to the sun's position in the sky at your location. He thought that in the motions of the moons of Jupiter he had an absolute time-piece in the sky. Using his accurate tables he could record the time when any of those moons moved into Jupiter's shadow. If a ship's captain observed a particular eclipse, he would know the time in Florence. Comparing it with his local time (though he would have to adjust his inaccurate mechanical clock every day), he could get a good idea of the difference in the two times. From that difference he could calculate his longitude.

However, the captain would find it difficult to observe Jupiter's moons from the rolling, pitching deck of his ship. Galileo tried to devise ways of keeping a telescope steady, but never achieved much success. Nonetheless, he spent a lot of time trying to sell his idea to the governments of Spain and Holland.

During the year after Galileo's *Bodies in Water* appeared, he noted the objections the philosophers were publishing against it. Three of them were professors at Pisa; the fourth was Ludovico delle Colombe. Galileo criticized their arguments and ridiculed them for clinging to Aristotle. Galileo passed his numerous notes to Benedetto Castelli, his friend and former student. Castelli compiled them all and had them published in 1615. This *Reply to Oppositions* had many more pages than either Galileo's original work or the sum of the four pamphlets by his critics.

In March 1616, church authorities in Rome suspended Copernicus's book, *On the Revolutions of the Celestial Spheres.* That is, they forbade Catholics to read the book until it had been "corrected." The events that led to this ban on Copernicus will be described in chapter 5. Although the ban did not mention Galileo, everyone considered it to have been directed against him. As a result, he abandoned his activities promoting the idea that the earth moves. At the same time, Jesuit mathematicians considered that their position had been strengthened. Two years

Fridericí Achillis Ducis Wirtemberg. Confultátio de Principatu inter Provincias Europæ, habita Tubingæ in Illuftri Collegio , anno Chrifti 1613.

Donelli Enucleati , *five* Commentariorum Hugonis Donelli de Iure Civili in compendium ita redactorum, *&c.*

Et quia etiam ad notitiam præfatæ Sacræ Congregationis pervenit, falfam illam doctrinam Pythagoricam , divinæque Scripturæ omnino adverfantem de mobilitate Terræ,& immobilitate Solis , quam Nicolaus Copernicus de revolutionibus orbium cæleftium , & Didacus Aftunica in Iob etiam docent , jam divulgari , & à multis recipi, ficuti videre'eft ex quadam epiftola impreffa cuiufdam Patris Carmelitæ , cui titulus ; *Lettera del Reu. Padre Maeftro Paolo Antonio Fofcarini Carmelitano fopra l'opinione de' Pittagorici , e del Copernico , della mobilità della Terra , e ftabilità del Sole ; & Il nuovo Pittagorico Siftema del Mondo, in Napoli per Lazzaro Scoriggio* 1615. in qua dictus Pater oftendere conatur,præfatam doctrinam de immobilitate folis in centro Mundi, & mobilitate Terræ,confonam effe veritati , & non adverfari Sacræ Scripturæ : Ideò ne vlterius huiufmodi opinio in perniciem Catholicæ veritatis ferpat , cenfuit dictos, Nicolaum Copernicum de Revolutionibus orbium , & Didacum Aftunica in Iob fufpendendos effe donec corrigantur. Librum verò Patris Pauli Antonij Fofcarini Carmelitæ, omnino prohibendum,atque damnandum, aliofque omnes Libros pariter idem docentes, prohibendos , prout præfenti Decreto omnes refpective prohibet, damnat,atque fufpendit. In quorum fidem præfens Decretum manu, & figillo Illuftriffimi, & Reverendiffimi D. Cardinalis Sanctæ Cæciliæ Epifcopi Albanen. fignatum,& munitum fuit , *die* 5. *Martij* 1616.

P. Epif. Albanen. Card. Sanct. Cæciliæ.

Locus † figilli.

Regift. fol. 90.

later, they found a way to assert their superiority in astronomy.

The occasion came in the autumn of 1618, when three comets appeared in the sky in quick succession. Superstitious people considered them to be portents of disaster. Astronomers tried to explain them. Jesuit mathematicians at the Roman College studied the comets with great care. They gathered information about their appearance from other Jesuits across Europe and held public meetings in Rome to announce their findings. They promoted the idea that the comets were planetlike objects located beyond the moon. The Jesuits published their results in the report of a speech by Orazio Grassi, chief mathematician at the Roman College. Grassi said the comets showed a very small parallax, which meant they were far from the earth.

In this ruling from 1616 church authorities placed Copernicus's revolutionary book, On the Revolutions of the Celestial Spheres, *on the list of books Catholics were forbidden to read.*

At the same time, a number of people wrote Galileo asking for his opinion about the comets. Again bedridden by rheumatism and fever, he did not respond for a while. After Grassi's speech was published, Galileo and his friends decided that they could not let the Jesuits take over the leading role in astronomy. Until then, Galileo had clearly been the paramount astronomical observer in Europe.

Galileo wrote a reply to Grassi and had it published in the name of his close associate, Mario Guiducci. Galileo declared that parallax was worthless in locating the comets as long as their nature remained unknown. Perhaps, he wrote, they are reflections of sunlight from vapors high in the atmosphere. If so, they would not show parallax.

Galileo was also critical of a suggestion by Grassi that the telescope showed that comets were far away. Grassi had said this because the telescope did not enlarge comets, just as it did not enlarge stars. In contrast, the telescope did make planets (which were much closer than the stars) appear as tiny discs; that is, enlarged from points of light as seen by the naked eye.

Galileo poked fun at Grassi for thinking that the telescope could be used to measure distances. At this point Grassi became thoroughly annoyed with Galileo. Perhaps he thought that the ban on Copernicus would have silenced the Florentine. So Grassi quickly published a 70-page attack on the ideas of Galileo that Guiducci had reported. Grassi's book was called *The Astronomical Balance: Weighing Galileo's Opinions on Comets*. Grassi did not identify himself as the author. He attributed it to a fictitious pupil of his, whom he called Lotario Sarsi. Grassi went through the Guiducci report point by point, raising every objection he could think of.

Galileo's Roman friends, especially in the Lincean Academy, urged Galileo to reply in kind. He delayed for several years. Finally, in October 1622, three years after the controversy had begun, Galileo sent his completed manuscript to the Linceans for them to publish in Rome.

Galileo picked up on Grassi's metaphor of the balance. He called his book *The Assayer,* referring to the delicate balances used to weigh precious metals to a fraction of a grain. In Guiducci's report, Galileo had criticized Grassi for following many of Tycho Brahe's astronomical "fantasies." A Danish astronomer, Tycho (known by his first name, like Leonardo and Galileo) made the best astronomical observations before the invention of the telescope. He also proposed a planetary scheme with the earth in the center, the sun circulating around the earth, and the planets orbiting the sun.

Galileo had also derided Grassi for referring to the opinions of poets about comets. In *The Balance,* Sarsi denied that Grassi had followed Tycho in anything except how to locate comets. He wrote:

> in nothing else was Tycho followed. Even with his telescope, the lynx-eyed astrologer [Galileo] cannot look into the inner thoughts of the mind. But suppose we grant that my master followed Tycho. How much of a crime is that? Whom might he follow instead? Ptolemy? whose followers' throats are threatened by the out-thrust sword of Mars now made closer. Or Copernicus? All who are dutiful will call everyone away from him, and reject and spurn his recently condemned hypothesis. . . .
>
> I would never have expected that courteous gentleman [Galileo] to reply scornfully that nature takes no delight in poetry. How far am I from that opinion! I have always considered nature as poetry. Nature seldom produces apples and other fruits without also putting forth flowers for our pleasure. Who would believe Galileo to be so harsh as to order such pleasant things, spicing serious matters, to be kept far away?

Galileo's response in *The Assayer* was equally cutting. Although he wrote to Sarsi, everyone knew that Orazio Grassi, chief mathematician of the Roman College, was hiding behind Sarsi's mask. Where Galileo used the word *philosophize,* he really meant *do science.*

It seems that Sarsi believes that to philosophize you must base yourself on the opinion of some celebrated author. Perhaps he thinks philosophy is a book of fiction created by some man, like Homer's *Iliad*—in such books, what is least important is whether what they say is true. Well, Signor Sarsi, that's not how things are. Philosophy is written in this grand book—I mean the universe—which is always open to our gaze. But it cannot be understood unless you first learn the language it's written in. It is written in the language of mathematics. Its characters are triangles, circles, and other figures. Without these it is humanly impossible to understand a single word of it. Without them you wander around in a pitch-black maze.

Galileo was being extremely sarcastic in telling an eminent mathematician that he had to use mathematics in order to understand science.

Another passage illustrates Galileo's derisive style. Grassi had supported Aristotle's claim that friction with the air would heat an arrow shot at high speed. He quoted three poets to support the idea. Then he reported a historical account that claimed Babylonian soldiers cooked eggs by whirling them through the air in slings.

Galileo mocked Grassi's piling up of authorities:

Reasoning is not like carrying a load, where several horses can carry more sacks of grain than one alone. Reasoning is more like running—one Arabian steed will outrun a hundred pack horses.

Then Galileo turned to the Babylonians:

If Sarsi wants, I'll believe that Babylonians cooked eggs by whirling them rapidly in slings. But the cause is very different from what he says. I reason as follows: "If we cannot achieve an effect claimed for others, we must lack something they had. And if we lack only one thing, that must have been the cause. We do not lack eggs, or slings, or sturdy fellows to whirl them. Yet that does not cook eggs. In fact, if they're already hot, whirling will cool them. What we do lack is being Babylonian. Therefore, being Babylonian was the cause of cooking the eggs."

Galileo's *Assayer* was widely praised as a literary master-piece. It effectively restored his prestige as a court scientist to be reckoned with. It also appeared at what seemed to be an auspicious time for Galileo and his Lincean friends. Just as the printing was being completed, a new pope ascended the throne of Peter. He was Urban VIII, Galileo's old friend, Maffeo Barberini. The Linceans dedicated *The Assayer* to the new pope. At the same time, *The Assayer*'s success helped turn the Jesuits into dangerous enemies.

Galileo on Trial

Wednesday, June 22, 1633. The Dominican convent of Santa Maria sopra Minerva in Rome. A white-robed penitent kneels before seven Cardinal-Inquisitors and reads a prepared confession:

> I, Galileo, son of the late Vincenzio Galilei of Florence, seventy years of age, . . . swear that I have always believed, and will continue to believe all that the Holy Catholic and Apostolic Church holds, preaches, and teaches. . . .
>
> I have been judged strongly suspected of heresy, in having held and believed that the sun is motionless in the center of the world, and the earth is not the center and moves. . . .
>
> With a sincere heart and unfeigned faith, I abjure, curse, and detest the above-named errors and heresies. . . I swear that in future I will never again say or assert, orally or in writing, anything that might cause a similar suspicion about me.

How had Galileo arrived at this sorry state? To answer this question we must go back to the year 1610. In that year, Galileo had become philosopher at the court of the grand duke of Tuscany. He used that position to promote new ways of doing philosophy—what we today call science.

A 17th-century engraving shows a public recantation before the Roman Inquisition in the church of Santa Maria sopra Minerva in Rome, the same church where Galileo was forced to recant his views on the motion of the earth.

As court philosopher, Galileo displaced others who had adhered to the traditions of Aristotle. They did not take kindly to being pushed aside. And in the controversy over floating, they became even more annoyed at being ridiculed for the sake of entertaining the Tuscan court.

Besides that, Galileo had some influence at the court. In mid-1613, he persuaded Cosimo II to appoint his colleague Benedetto Castelli as professor of mathematics at the University of Pisa. A sign of the uneasiness of the traditionalists appeared very quickly. An overseer of the university warned Castelli that he should not teach the Copernican idea of the earth's motions. Castelli assured him he would not, and that Galileo had already given him the same advice.

In December of that year, when the court had moved to Pisa for the winter, Castelli was invited to have breakfast with the grand duke and his family. After the meal they retired to the drawing room of Cosimo's mother, the grand duchess Christina. There she began to question Castelli about whether the idea that the earth moved contradicted the Bible. Castelli guessed that she had been influenced by another one of the guests, Professor Cosimo Boscaglia, a traditional philosopher.

When Castelli told Galileo this, he wrote back a long letter, setting forth his own opinion that science and religion should not be mixed. He considered that God had authored both the Holy Scriptures and the Book of Nature. They are both equally true, he said.

But, Galileo claimed, sometimes the language in the Bible has been adjusted to suit common understanding. It may appear to say the earth does not move, but that is only because in ordinary experience it seems that way. On the other hand, there are no such adjustments in Nature. If Nature can show us that the earth moves, then we must not doubt it. And we must not allow the Bible to contradict what Nature shows plainly to our minds by sensible experiences and conclusive proofs.

Galileo referred to a famous passage in the Old Testament that was often used to dispute the earth's motions. Joshua was in a battle and needed a longer day to finish off his enemies. He prayed to the Lord to stop the sun's motion across the sky for a while. And God complied: "The sun stood still and the moon halted until a nation had taken vengeance on its enemies. . . . The sun stayed in mid heaven and made no haste to set for almost a whole day" (Joshua 10:13).

Galileo's opponents had used this passage to support the views of Aristotle and Ptolemy. But Galileo said that in their systems, the daily motion did not belong to the sun alone, but to all the heavenly bodies. And it was driven by an outer sphere called the Prime Mobile. So, for their systems to be true, Joshua should have asked God to stop the Prime Mobile. Since the Bible had Joshua say something else, the Bible was accommodating itself to the ordinary understanding of the people, who had never heard of the Prime Mobile.

However, the Copernican system could fit Joshua's actual words. Since the sun rotates on its axis about once a month, perhaps that motion controls all the planets. Then, stopping the sun's rotation might also stop the earth's rotation. And that would cause the day to be lengthened.

Castelli made several copies of Galileo's letter and distributed it to friends. One of them fell into the hands of Galileo's enemies in the Pigeon League. Nothing more happened for a year. But in December 1614, the league found a priest to preach against Galileo and his theory of the motions of the earth. Tommaso Caccini, a Dominican, took as his text the passage about Joshua. He explained it in the traditional way. He also took the occasion to denounce mathematicians as enemies of the true faith. With this sermon, the members of the Pigeon League made a major shift in their tactics against Galileo. Since they had not been able to discredit him in philosophy, they turned to religion.

Less than two months after Caccini's sermon, a fellow Dominican in Florence, Father Niccolò Lorini, sent a copy of Galileo's letter to Castelli to the Inquisition in Rome. Lorini said the Dominicans felt the letter contained heretical statements against the Christian faith.

The Inquisitors sent the letter to a theological consultant. He considered the letter not to be heretical. However, in March 1615, Caccini went to Rome to testify before the Inquisition. He explicitly charged that Galileo believed that the sun was at rest in the center of the universe, and that the earth rotated and revolved about it. He said Galileo had written such things in his *Letters on Sunspots,* which was not true. Caccini made other charges, which the Inquisition also investigated. They found them to be baseless.

Galileo got wind of these Inquisition proceedings and began to worry. He wrote to friends in Rome seeking advice about what he should do. Generally, they told him to be careful, and to avoid asserting the reality of the earth's motions.

Then, in March 1615, a priest from Naples named Paolo Foscarini published a pamphlet claiming that the Copernican system should not be considered contrary to the Bible. Galileo received a copy of Foscarini's work and was encouraged by it. Another copy went to Cardinal Roberto Bellarmino, a leading Jesuit theologian and a member of the Roman Inquisition.

Bellarmino wrote a letter to Foscarini with a copy to Galileo. He assured them they would have no trouble if they treated the earth's motions only hypothetically. He added that it would be dangerous to assert that the earth really moves, for that would harm Christian faith by contradicting the Bible. If the earth's motion was proved, Bellarmino said, then the Church would say that passages in the Bible that seem contrary are not understood, rather than that the earth's motion is false. He concluded that he knew of no proof that the earth moves.

In response, Galileo expanded his letter to Castelli. Addressing it to Cosimo's mother, the grand duchess Christina, Galileo gave many details of how he thought Nature and the Bible should be interpreted. In particular, he urged that the authority of the Bible be limited to matters of faith and morals.

Galileo quoted a friend of Bellarmino's, who had said, "The purpose of Holy Scriptures is to tell us how to go to heaven, not how the heavens go." Bellarmino, on the other hand, had written that all statements in the Bible were matters of faith because they came directly from the Holy Spirit.

Cardinal Roberto Bellarmino, a leading Jesuit theologian, cautioned Galileo against asserting that the earth moves. Bellarmino refused to support scientific results that seemed to contradict the Bible.

Galileo's chronic illnesses confined him to bed through most of 1615. But by December he felt well enough to travel, and he decided to go to Rome. He wanted to know whether the authorities were preparing to charge him with heresy. If not, he wanted to protect the Church from serious error, in case it wanted to condemn the Copernican system. He felt that the Church could become a laughingstock if it ruled against the earth's motions, which might later be proved to be real.

In Rome, Galileo found that important officials were much cooler toward him than they had been in 1611. However, he soon felt that he personally was out of danger. And so he began attending gatherings where he demonstrated the plausibility of the Copernican system.

Copernicus had suggested that the earth could be moving even though we do not feel it. It was similar to the situation of being on a ship just leaving the dock: though you know the ship is moving, it looks like the dock is moving away from the ship. Opponents of Copernicus, including Cardinal Bellarmino, replied that the example was worthless. That was because we know that the dock (which is attached to the earth) is at rest, and so can correct the illusion of its motion.

Galileo replied that such an argument begged the question. We do not really know whether the sun or the earth is in motion. Hence we should consider them as two ships on the sea. Whichever ship we are on will feel at rest, while the other will appear to move. To know which is really moving requires other evidence.

Another standard objection to the motion of the earth came from the fact that a stone dropped from a tower falls vertically to the foot of the tower. If the earth moved eastward at hundreds of miles per hour, Aristotelians claimed, the stone would fall far to the west of the tower. They claimed as evidence that a stone dropped from the mast of a moving ship would fall far astern of the ship.

Galileo argued that was not the way things happened. Suppose the ship is moving forward at 15 feet each second. While held at the top of the mast, the stone at the masthead would also be moving at 15 feet per second. If the stone took 2 seconds to fall to the deck, the boat would move 30 feet forward while it fell. But so would the stone!

As a result, the stone would still strike the deck at the foot of the mast. Galileo claimed to have performed the experiment. Nonetheless, he argued that reason alone should demonstrate the truth of his claim. On numerous occasions, Galileo's logic overwhelmed his audience. But it did not convince his opponents.

Galileo also presented his argument that the tides depended on the motions of the earth. He wrote it out and gave it to a friendly young cardinal, Alessandro Orsini, hoping he might convince others. But the move backfired. Cardinal Orsini (who was just 22 years old) mentioned Galileo's concerns to Pope Paul V in public. The pope was outraged and told him the Inquisition was handling the matter. In fact, just then the Inquisition had sent two propositions to a dozen theologians for their opinion. The propositions had not been found in Galileo's *Letters on Sunspots,* but were taken from Caccini's testimony of the previous spring.

Both propositions were condemned, in the following terms:

1. *The sun is in the center of the world and completely devoid of motion.* This proposition is foolish and absurd in philosophy. It is formally heretical since it explicitly contradicts the Bible in many places, according to the literal meaning of the words and the common interpretation and understanding of the Holy Fathers.

2. *The earth is not the center of the world nor motionless, but moves as a whole and with daily rotation.* This proposition receives the same judgment in philosophy, and is at least erroneous in faith.

Pope Paul V commanded strict obedience to all the church's rules and showed only mild interest in Galileo's science.

Many people contend that those theologians had no business judging the propositions philosophically. Nonetheless, the theologians did express their opinion that the propositions smelled of heresy because they contradicted the Bible. Since their opinion was expressed in a report to the Inquisition, it did not constitute an official stand by the Catholic Church.

However, as a result of this opinion, two actions followed. First, Foscarini's book was put on the *Index of Prohibited Books.* That meant that Catholics were forbidden to read it. Also Copernicus's book was prohibited until it was corrected according to instructions that church officials would provide.

The second action was directed against Galileo. The pope instructed Cardinal Bellarmino to call Galileo in and warn him to abandon Copernicus. If he refused, he was to be commanded never again to speak or write about the Copernican system. If he refused to obey that order, he should be imprisoned.

The next day, Friday, February 26, 1616, Cardinal Bellarmino ordered Galileo to his residence and gave him the warning. According to one document in the files of the Inquisition, Galileo agreed without protest to abandon his Copernican opinions.

However, there is another document that suggests that the second command was also given. That is, that Galileo was ordered to abandon the Copernican opinion and never again "to hold, teach, or defend it in any way whatever, whether orally or in writing." This document represents itself to be minutes of the meeting with Cardinal Bellarmino. But it contains no signatures to attest that what it says actually happened.

The following week, Galileo had a long audience with the pope. Writing about it later, Galileo said that the pope "consoled me that I could live with my mind at peace, for I was so regarded by His Holiness and the whole congregation that they would not easily listen to my slanderers, and that I could feel safe as long as he lived."

Galileo stayed on in Rome until the end of May. Before he left, he obtained a signed certificate from Cardinal Bellarmino. In it, the cardinal affirmed that Galileo had received no punishments. He had simply been informed of the declaration in the *Index of Prohibited Books* that the doctrine of Copernicus "is contrary to Holy Scripture, and therefore cannot be defended or held." Galileo filed this certificate with his important papers. He took it to mean that he could discuss the Copernican system hypothetically, but not claim it to be real.

Galileo returned to Florence and resumed studying longitudes and motion, although he was frequently afflicted with rheumatic pains. In 1621, Cosimo II died, and was succeeded by his 11-year-old son Ferdinando II.

Until 1627, Tuscany was ruled by his mother, the arch-duchess, and his grandmother, Grand Duchess Christina. Galileo feared they would not support him as firmly as Cosimo had.

Then, in 1623, there occurred what Galileo called a "marvelous conjuncture." Just when the Linceans had *The Assayer* ready to publish, a new pope was elected. In August, Cardinal Maffeo Barberini become Pope Urban VIII. Several of Galileo's Lincean friends belonged to Barberini's retinue and were promoted to serve the new pope. They immediately arranged to dedicate *The Assayer* to Urban.

The pope was thrilled by the elegant writing. That encouraged Galileo and the Linceans to think that they could enhance their reputation at the expense of the Jesuits. They sought Urban's patronage to support their scientific philosophy in preference to the traditions of Aristotle.

Galileo traveled to Rome in the spring of 1624 to pay homage to the new pope. Over several weeks, he was granted six audiences with Urban. Galileo inquired whether the ban on Copernicus might be lifted. Although Urban said he had opposed it back in 1616, he would not change it now. Nevertheless, Galileo obtained the pope's permission to write about the Copernican system by comparing it to Ptolemy's.

The pope expected Galileo to produce another witty book to titillate courtly sensibilities. But on no account should it appear to make motions of the earth real. Urban knew about Galileo's theory of the tides. A pretty fantasy, he thought. However, Galileo should make it clear that Almighty God could produce the tides in any number of ways. No one should suppose that frail human intellects could comprehend the mysteries of God's actions.

Galileo returned to Florence with the pope's praises ringing in his ears. He immediately set out to produce a great work. He composed a dialogue among three characters to explore the details of the Copernican hypothesis.

Wearing the mask of Copernicus was Salviati, Galileo's great good friend in Florence. To represent the Aristotelians, Galileo named a character Simplicio, after an ancient commentator on Aristotle. Readers could be forgiven for thinking of this character as a simpleton. The third character, named for Galileo's Venetian friend, Sagredo, represented men of common sense. From 1625 to 1630, Galileo referred to the book as "my Dialogue on the Tides." He set the stage for exploring the hypotheses of the earth's motions, which could explain the tides. He identified the four sections of the book as days of conversation among his three characters.

In the first day, Galileo dealt with the general structure of the universe and the experimental and logical processes needed to understand it. Salviati described the various discoveries of "our friend, the Lincean Academician," that is, Galileo himself. Here and throughout the book, Salviati attacked and made fun of numerous Aristotelian arguments. Indeed, there are many more references in it to Aristotle than to Ptolemy.

In the second day, Galileo had Salviati argue that no direct evidence could be found to decide whether the earth did or did not rotate on its axis. He claimed that all the observations we make of things moving on the earth would be just the same in either case.

In the third day, Galileo concentrated on astronomical phenomena. He showed the Copernican arrangement to be at least as plausible as the Ptolemaic. Indeed, he seemed to show that the Copernican system is simpler and easier to understand.

He also used the paths of sunspots across the sun's face to show that the sun's axis of rotation was tilted from the plane of the earth's orbit. This gave him another argument for showing that an earth in motion made the system simpler. By now Galileo had shown that none of the arguments against the earth's motions can be supported absolutely. That

Galileo created a conver-
sation among three
fictional characters on
principles of natural philosophy for his Dialogue.
The characters—seen
here on the frontispiece
—represent a questioner,
a follower of Aristotle,
and a follower of
Copernicus.

allowed him to devote the fourth day to explaining the
tides. If the earth rotates on its axis once a day and revolves
about the sun once a year, then the combination of these
motions could shake the earth and make tidal motions in
oceans and seas.

In 1630, Galileo took his finished manuscript to Rome
to be approved by church authorities. The chief censor read
it and gave tentative approval, if certain changes were made.
In particular, the censor said that the pope refused to allow
the tides to be mentioned in the title. As a result, Galileo

text continues on page 90

The planetary scheme of Copernicus has a particular advantage over Ptolemy's in the way it accounts for a peculiar motion of planets. About once a year, Mars, Jupiter, and Saturn seem to trace out a looping path against the background of the stars. The figure below shows such a loop for Mars. The solid line shows the path of Mars from September 3, 1996, to September 18, 1997. Between February 10 and June 30, 1997, Mars seems to stop, reverse direction, stop again, and then resume its forward motion.

Ptolemy, with his earth-centered system, had to make a special provision for this looping motion. He did it by having Mars revolve on the circumference of a circle whose center revolved about the earth. Another astronomer, Tycho Brahe, identified the center of the smaller circle with the sun.

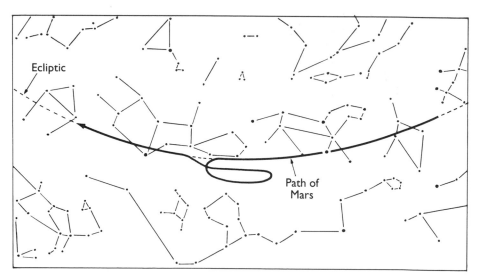

When Mars (or Jupiter or Saturn) is highest in the sky at midnight, the sun is exactly opposite on the other side of the earth. At such times, Mars appears to move in the reverse of its normal motion relative to the stars. Then, after resuming its normal motion, it appears to have followed a looping path.

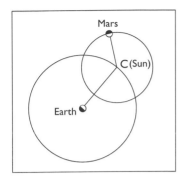

When Copernicus made the earth a planet in orbit about the sun, he found that the looping motion of Mars followed naturally from his new arrangement. The looping motion is not real, but only apparent. It results from the fact that the earth is traveling around the sun faster than Mars. Running on an inside track, earth catches up to Mars, passes it, and then leaves it behind.

Galileo described all this in a clever passage in his *Dialogue*. Salviati is speaking to Simplicio.

What are we to say of the apparent movement of a planet, so uneven that it not only goes fast at one time and slow at another, but sometimes stops entire-

ly and even goes backward a long way after that? To save these appearances, Ptolemy introduces vast epicycles, adapting them one by one to each planet, with certain rules about incongruous motions—all of which can be done away with by one very simple motion of the earth. Do you not think it extremely absurd, Simplicio, that in Ptolemy's construction where all planets are assigned their own orbits, one above another, it should be necessary to say that Mars, placed above the sun's sphere, often . . . gets closer to the earth than the body of the sun is, and then a little later soars immeasurably above it? These and other anomalies are cured by a single and simple movement of the earth.

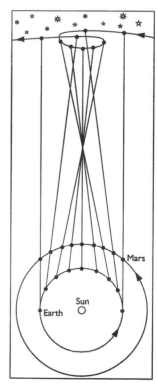

Salviati then went on to describe Copernicus's explanation of the looping motion of a planet as shown in the figure on the right.

simply titled the book *Dialogue,* by "Galileo Galilei, Lincean; distinguished Mathematician of the University of Pisa; and Philosopher and Chief Mathematician of His Serene Highness, the Grand Duke of Tuscany." He added a rambling description of the contents, a part of which some people soon took to be part of the title: "On the two Chief World Systems, Ptolemaic and Copernican."

In response to concerns of the censor, Galileo also changed the structure of the book in subtle ways. Originally, he had intended it to be one long argument—if the earth moves with a double motion, then it could cause the tides. To stress the tides less, that form almost disappeared. Instead, Galileo appeared to be trying to destroy all objections to Copernicus, and to be using his tidal theory as clinching proof of the earth's motions.

The Linceans were supposed to publish the book in Rome, with the censor approving the final version page by page as it went to the printer. Galileo returned to Florence to complete the revisions. Then, in August 1630, Prince Cesi died. Since he had supplied all the funds for the Lincean Academy, it could no longer afford to pay for the publication of Galileo's *Dialogue.*

Also at that time, the bubonic plague raged through northern Italy. To try to prevent the plague from spreading southward, officials erected customs barriers. They thoroughly fumigated every piece of luggage. Galileo hesitated to send his manuscript to Rome if every page of it had to be held over a smoking fire. In addition, Castelli, now in Rome as papal mathematician, warned that Galileo's enemies were still active. They might interfere with the *Dialogue*'s publication there. Galileo decided to publish in Florence.

He got permission from the Roman censor to do that. However, the book would have to be reviewed by authorities in Florence. And the censor would send two important items to be included. These were the preface and a closing statement. The censor had revised the preface to make the tides appear less prominent. And the closing statement included the pope's assertion that God's power could not be limited by human minds.

With those changes made, Galileo sent the book to the printer in Florence in August 1631. A thousand printed copies appeared in February 1632. As expected, the *Dialogue* thrilled Galileo's friends and appalled his enemies. But entirely unexpectedly, Pope Urban switched sides. By September 1632, the supreme pontiff, previously a keen patron, had become Galileo's implacable foe.

What had happened? No one knows for sure. Historians are still speculating on the pope's about-face. Probably a variety of circumstances combined to change the pope's mind about Galileo.

At this stage of the religious wars in Germany, the pope sided with France and Sweden against Spain and the emperor in Prague. Since Sweden was Protestant, Spanish cardinals attacked the pope's policy. A member of his own staff, a good friend of Galileo's, seemed to be supporting the Spaniards. Urban VIII felt he was surrounded by enemies and in danger of being impeached.

The death of Prince Cesi in 1630 had disarrayed the Lincean Academy. Their anti-Jesuit campaign faltered. The Jesuits took advantage of that situation to restore their influence. They claimed that in favoring motions of the earth, the *Dialogue* lent support to the Protestants. One Jesuit, Christoph Scheiner, had a particular grievance against the *Dialogue*. He claimed that Galileo had stolen information about sunspots from him, though that was untrue.

DIALOGO
D I
GALILEO GALILEI LINCEO
MATEMATICO SOPRAORDINARIO
DELLO STVDIO DI PISA.
E Filofofo, e Matematico primario del
SERENISSIMO
GR.DVCA DI TOSCANA.
Doue ne i congreffi di quattro giornate fi difcorre
fopra i due
MASSIMI SISTEMI DEL MONDO
TOLEMAICO, E COPERNICANO;
*Proponendo indeterminatamente le ragioni Filofofiche, e Naturali
tanto per l'vna, quanto per l'altra parte.*

CON PRI   VILEGI.

IN FIORENZA, Per Gio:Batifta Landini MDCXXXII.
CON LICENZA DE' SVPERIORI.

Galileo's Dialogue, published in 1632, provoked leaders of the Catholic Church because it appeared to violate the 1616 ban on spreading the ideas of Copernicus.

Finally, the pope's statement about God's power had been put in the mouth of Simplicio in the *Dialogue*. Someone whispered into Urban's ear that Galileo had thereby made fun of him. In mid-August, the pope ordered a special committee to investigate whether the *Dialogue* should be banned. A month later, the committee reported to the Inquisition that Galileo should be called to account.

In their investigations, the committee had found the minute in Galileo's file that said he had been ordered never again to mention the earth's motions. As a result, they claimed, he should be tried for disobeying that command. The Inquisition, with the pope at its head, ordered Galileo to come to Rome. Illness delayed his trip for some months. Finally, the pope commanded immediate obedience. Otherwise, he would send troops to bring Galileo to Rome in chains.

Galileo left Florence on January 20, 1633. After two weeks' quarantine halfway along, he arrived in Rome on February 13. The pope at least allowed him to live at the Tuscan embassy, rather than putting him in prison. The pope may have had more regard for the Grand Duke of Tuscany than for Galileo himself.

The Inquisition delayed action for two months. Probably they wanted Galileo to stew for a while. Then, on Tuesday, April 12, the Inquisition took Galileo into custody. He was interrogated the same day. Preliminary questioning established that Galileo had been called to Rome to answer charges related to his *Dialogue*. Then the questioners dropped their bombshell:

> Does he recall that in Rome in 1616, he was commanded, in the presence of witnesses, not to hold, defend or teach the Copernican opinion in any way whatsoever?

Galileo did not recall it:

> I have relied on this certificate given to me by Lord Cardinal Bellarmino. It says that I may not hold or defend the said opinion. But the words "not to teach," and "in

any way whatsoever," strike me as new. The certificate does not mention them.

He also claimed that in the *Dialogue* he neither held nor defended the opinion of the earth's motion. Indeed, he said, "In that book I showed the contrary, that Copernicus's reasons are invalid and inconclusive."

None of the inquisitors would believe that. In fact, they had three theologians write reports about the *Dialogue*. All three agreed that Galileo actually had defended Copernicus; and further, they strongly suspected that he held the condemned opinion. Nonetheless, the inquisitors were shocked to hear of Cardinal Bellarmino's certificate—they had no inkling of its existence.

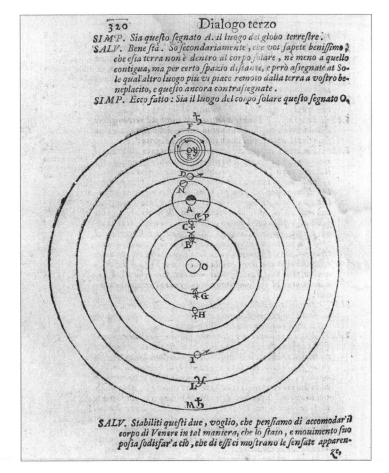

This diagram from Galileo's Dialogue clearly shows the Copernican system—the sun at the center of the universe, with the planets (and their newly discovered moons) revolving around it.

Galileo never said what had actually happened back on February 26, 1616. He did not have to. He had Bellarmino's certificate, duly signed, which clearly implied that he had not been given any special command. Even if the minutes in the file correctly described the events of that day, they had no legal standing because they were not signed. Further, if officials wanted to check, they could find Cardinal Bellarmino's report to the Inquisition that Galileo had accepted the simple warning.

The inquisitors thus could not lean as heavily as they had intended on the command not to teach Copernicus's views in any way whatsoever. Instead, they used the three theologians' reports to show that Galileo had also disobeyed the general prohibition against teaching that the earth moved.

The inquisitors kept Galileo in custody—not in a prison cell, but in a small, comfortable apartment in their own building. Two weeks after the first interview, they managed to find something to which Galileo could confess. Galileo admitted to having made arguments for the earth's motions stronger than he had intended: "My error was one of vain ambition, pure ignorance, and inadvertence," he confessed.

Now Galileo was allowed to return to the Tuscan embassy, where he was ministered to by the ambassador and his kindly wife. Ten days later Galileo submitted his defense. He argued that he had not been intentionally disobedient. Since the Roman censor had licensed his book, he felt that it must not have infringed the rules of the *Index of Prohibited Books.*

At worst, Galileo seems to have been half-guilty of two crimes: (1) of disobeying a direct command, even though evidence for the command came from a dubious document; and (2) of publishing a book that broke the rules of the *Index,* even though the Roman censor had given his permission. In most modern courts, lack of full proof of either crime would have led to his release. But the pope was determined to get some kind of conviction. The Jesuits seemed to demand it.

The pope and the cardinals of the Inquisition dithered for more than a month. Then, on June 16, 1633, they decided that a half plus a half should add up to a whole crime—and they put the *Dialogue* on the *Index* and convicted Galileo of second-degree suspicion of heresy. Galileo felt as if his name had been inscribed in the book of the dead.

Galileo summarized the next year of his life in a letter to a friend. He wrote that after the trial he was sent back to the Tuscan embassy. Then the Inquisition allowed him to spend five months in Siena as guest of his good friend Archbishop Ascanio Piccolomini. There he received a letter from his loving daughter, Virginia (Sister Maria Celeste):

> There are two pigeons in the dovecote waiting for you to come and eat them. There are beans in the garden waiting for you to gather them. Your tower is lamenting your long absence.
>
> When you were in Rome I said to myself, if he were but at Siena! Now you are at Siena, I say, would he were at Arcetri! But God's will be done!

The kindly archbishop restored Galileo to life. Paying little attention to the Inquisition, he invited leading Sienese citizens to visit Galileo. Their scientific conversations encouraged Galileo to begin writing his next book.

In December, the Inquisition sent Galileo home to his little villa in Arcetri, south of Florence. He regularly visited his daughters in their nearby convent. Virginia's health had declined from the stress of her father's troubles, and from her work in the convent's sickroom. She died of severe intestinal bleeding in early April 1634. Later that month Galileo wrote to an in-law:

> My health is very bad. I suffer much more from the rupture than has been true before. My pulse intermits and I

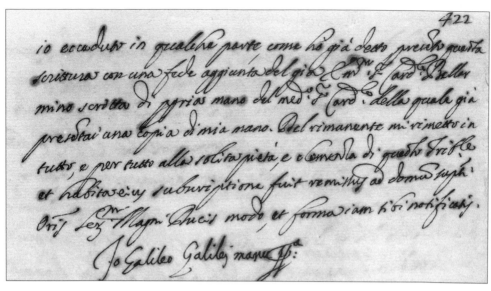

The final paragraph of Galileo's handwritten confession to the Inquisition. Galileo confessed to writing a book that supported Copernicus although he had been ordered not to.

often have violent palpitations of the heart. Then, the most profound melancholy comes over me; I have no appetite and loathe myself. I feel myself perpetually called by my beloved daughter.

Before the end of 1634, Galileo picked up the threads of his shattered life. Although he had lost the sight of one eye and the other one was weakening, he got back to work. During the next two years he completed his *Two New Sciences*. He wrote it all in Italian, except for his mathematical theorems on motion, which were in Latin.

Cast as a dialogue among the same three characters he had used before, the *Two New Sciences* represented Galileo's scientific testament. As he wrote, "Now the door has been opened to a new reflection, full of infinite and admirable conclusions, which in times to come will be able to exercise other creative minds."

The *Two New Sciences* uses its first "day" to introduce the topics of the other three days. At the opening, the three men discuss the problem of scale models. If built of the same materials, a ship scaled up a hundred times from a small model would collapse under its own weight. Galileo stressed that in the real world, geometry must be qualified by physics. He also applied the principle of scaling to animals.

Galileo devoted the second day to analyzing the strengths of beams—laying the scientific basis for civil and mechanical engineering.

The third and fourth days contained a treatise on accelerated motions and projectiles, written by "our Lincean Academician." Here Galileo presented the results of the studies in motion he had begun in 1602. Among the mathematical theorems, he interspersed "philosophical" discussions by his three characters.

Because of the Inquisition's prohibition, Galileo could not have his book printed in Italy. A friend in Germany found a

Galileo's daughter, Sister Marie Celeste, whose death in April 1634, combined with his own failing health, sent him into a deep depression.

patron willing to print the book, but the patron suddenly died and the project was abandoned. Galileo finally managed to find a Dutch publisher who would do the job. The book appeared in the summer of 1638.

By the time a copy arrived in Arcetri, Galileo could not see it. He had written to his friend, Elia Diodati, in Paris in January 1638, "Alas! revered Sir, your devoted friend and servant, Galileo, has been for a month totally and incurably blind. This heaven, this earth, this universe, which I have enlarged a hundred, nay, a thousand-fold beyond the limits previously accepted, are now shriveled up for me into that narrow compass occupied by my own person."

A young man named Vincenzio Viviani now came into Galileo's household to act as his secretary. From 1638

text continues on page 100

Compare two animals, such as a dog and a horse. If the linear dimensions (the height, breadth, and length) of the horse are three times those of the dog, then it will weigh 27 times as much. The table shows the approximate relative sizes of a medium-sized dog and a horse.

animal	height	weight
dog	1.5 feet	30 pounds
horse	4.5 feet	800 pounds

If the dog is scaled up to three times its dimensions, the strength of its bones would increase by no more than nine times. They could not support 27 times the original weight. So if you compare a foot bone of a horse with that of a dog, it will be immediately obvious that the horse's bones are proportionally much thicker.

The top figure on page 99 appears in the second "day" of Galileo's *Two New Sciences*. It shows an equivalent bone in two animals. The larger animal is three times bigger than the smaller one. The larger bone is three times as long but proportionally much thicker. That is because the larger animal is not 3 times but 27 times heavier than the smaller one. The bone must be much thicker to support all that weight. In the bottom figure on page 99, the smaller bone has been geometrically enlarged by a factor of three in all dimensions. According to Galileo's picture, the bone of the larger animal is 2.6 times thicker than this one.

Small animals are proportionally much stronger than larger ones. As Galileo wrote, "I believe that a little dog might carry on his back two or three dogs of the same size, whereas I doubt if a horse could carry even one horse of his own size." A bug can fall a distance many times its size without damage. A person, however, cannot safely fall more than a couple of times his height. You can realize, therefore, the physical impossibility of many monsters in the movies. A bug cannot be as big as a human without grossly

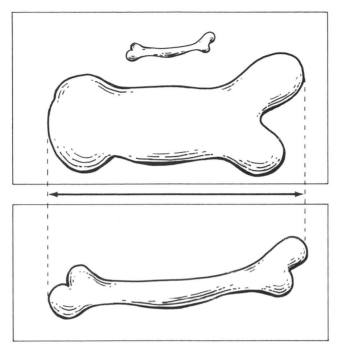

The top figure shows the equivalent bone in two different animals. The bottom figure shows that when the smaller bone is scaled up to the same length as the larger one, it is much thinner than the bone belonging to the heavier animal.

increasing the proportional thickness of its legs. The moviemakers only scale geometrically by photographic enlargement. They do not have to pay attention to the physical strengths that would actually be required.

As far as we know, Galileo was the first person to describe ideas about scaling in print.

Galileo's final published work, Two New Sciences, *was issued in 1638 by a Dutch publisher. Because of his problems with the Inquisition, Galileo was unable to find a printer in Italy willing to publish the book.*

DISCORSI
E
DIMOSTRAZIONI
MATEMATICHE,
intorno à due nuoue scienze,e
Attenenti·alla
MECANICA & i MOVIMENTI LOCALI,

del Signor
GALILEO GALILEI LINCEO,
Filosofo e Matematico primario del Serenissimo
Grand Duca di Toscana.

Con vna Appendice del centro di grauità d'alcuni Solidi.

IN LEIDA,
Appresso gli Elsevirii. M. D. C. XXXVIII.

to 1641, Galileo continued to correspond both with friends and rivals. Viviani read to him and wrote his letters. Some years later, he obtained the post of mathematician to the grand duke. He also sketched a biography of Galileo.

In the autumn of 1641 Galileo was confined to bed with palpitations of the heart and severe kidney pains. Feverish and unable to sleep, he knew that his end was near. He grieved that he was no longer allowed to drink wine, which he called "light held together by moisture."

Galileo died on the night of January 8, 1642. The grand duke requested permission to honor Galileo with a funeral oration and a marble monument. Urban VIII refused to allow either.

Galileo's body was laid to rest with little ceremony in a small crypt in a rear chapel of the church of Santa Croce in Florence. Only in 1737 did the Inquisition allow his remains to be transferred to the main part of the church. They were placed in a bronze and marble monument, funded by a bequest from Viviani, who lived until 1703. As he desired, his own remains were laid beside his master's.

The frontispiece to a 1656 collected edition of Galileo's works shows Galileo offering his telescope to the Muses while pointing to the sun, shown with the planets clearly revolving around it.

CHAPTER 6

Galileo in History

During the 1600s, physics went through several important transformations. At the beginning of the century, physics belonged to the natural philosophers in the universities. At the end, it belonged to experimenters in scientific societies. In between, mathematicians at princely courts delivered their discoveries as gifts to their patrons. Galileo played a major role in that transitional stage. He took physics out from under the dead weight of tradition. At the same time, he took the study of motion away from philosophy and gave it to mathematics.

Galileo began his career as a lowly, lonely mathematician at the University of Pisa. His philosophical colleague Francesco Buonamici published an analysis of all possible arguments about the causes of motion in a gigantic book of more than 1,000 pages. Published in 1591, *On Motion* was the last word in physics. In contrast, in 1638, the motion "days" in Galileo's *Two New Sciences* occupied only 130 pages.

At the university, Galileo had too low a status to be able to contradict the philosophers successfully. In 1610, he used his fortunate telescopic observations to gain membership in the court of Cosimo II of Florence. He named

Jupiter's moons for the Medici family and dedicated several of his books to the grand dukes. Aristocratic courts valued novelty in ways the universities did not. Galileo ornamented the Tuscan court and entertained it with scientific disputes. Although princes did not arbitrate the disputes, courtiers like Galileo chose subjects that would please their patrons.

Later, Urban VIII served as patron to Galileo—raised him up and then dropped him. His tribulations cautioned other scientists to distance themselves from princely patronage. Gradually, the warrant for scientific success moved from pleasing princes to producing incontestable experimental results.

In the 1660s two important scientific societies were founded. In England, promoters of the new experimental philosophy obtained a charter from King Charles II for the Royal Society of London. Although they admitted nonscientist noblemen as members, the scientists saw themselves more as members of a corporation than as clients of royal patrons. These scientists, mostly amateurs, were often physicians and clergymen. Their warrant for truth depended on experimental results, which they communicated in a regular publication. The *Philosophical Transactions of the Royal Society* was published monthly beginning in 1664. Such periodicals gradually replaced personal letters as the major way to announce new discoveries in science.

In France, Louis XIV funded the Academy of Sciences, with salaries for 15 members. Although the French government consulted the academicians from time to time, they considered themselves a corporation that set its own rules. They, too, announced their findings in a periodical publication.

Thus, during the 17th century the focus of scientific activity gradually progressed from university traditionalism, through courtly patronage, to self-governing scientific societies. As a courtly mathematician-philosopher, Galileo formed an essential link in this chain.

The pace of scientific inquiry had quickened even during Galileo's lifetime. In astronomy, Johannes Kepler made the major contribution. For much of his career, Kepler worked for the Holy Roman Emperor in Prague. Like Galileo, he was a courtier-mathematician.

Kepler's greatest achievement was to determine the orbit of the planet Mars quite precisely. Following the Copernican arrangement of the planets, Kepler found Mars's orbit to be elliptical, with the sun located at one focus of the ellipse. Kepler titled his book about the Mars orbit *The New Astronomy, or Celestial Physics.* However, the physics he applied to the planets was more like Aristotle's than Galileo's. Nonetheless, Kepler's interest in the causes of the motion of the planets started a trend that culminated in the work of Isaac Newton.

As Kepler paid little attention to Galileo's physics, so Galileo paid little attention to Kepler's astronomy. While they were friendly and admired each other, they were of very different temperaments. Kepler sought universal harmonies in the sky, while Galileo sought more limited rules for motions on earth. However, both men agreed in rejecting Aristotle's ideas about the absolute distinction between heaven and earth.

In 1635 Galileo's *Dialogue* was translated into Latin and published in a large edition. Three hundred copies arrived in Paris from the printer in Strasbourg. A circle of mathematicians in Paris read the book eagerly. At the center of this circle was a Catholic priest, Marin Mersenne. Sometimes called the post office of scientific Europe, Mersenne wrote numerous letters. He asked questions and communicated results among his many correspondents.

Galileo's work intrigued Mersenne immensely. He put Galileo's early treatise on mechanics into print for the first time in 1634—in a French translation. The same year, in another book, Mersenne summarized the first two days of Galileo's *Dialogue.* The long arm of the Inquisition did not reach as far as Paris.

Mersenne saw the manuscript of Galileo's *Two New Sciences* in the late fall of 1636 and published a very brief extract several months later. That was more than a year before Galileo's book itself was published. Then, in September 1638, Mersenne published a small book that summarized the whole of the *Two New Sciences*. Thus Mersenne helped to spread Galileo's ideas across Europe.

Mersenne's major correspondent was René Descartes. People today know Descartes for his mathematics and philosophy. Unlike Galileo, he eagerly adopted algebra and enriched it by inventing analytic geometry. This

DISCOURSES

CONCERNING

Two New Sciences

RELATING TO

Mechanicks and Local Motion,

IN

FOUR DIALOGUES.

I. Of the Refiftance of Solids againft Fraction.	III. Of Local Motion, *viz.* Equable, and naturally Accelerate.
II. Of the Caufe of their Coherence.	IV. Of Violent Motion, or of PROJECTS.

By GALILEO GALILEI,

Chief Philofopher *and* Mathematician *to the Grand Duke of* TUSCANY.

With an APPENDIX concerning the Center of Gravity of SOLID BODIES.

Done into *Englifh* from the *Italian*,

By THO. WESTON, *late Mafter, and now publifh'd by* JOHN WESTON, *prefent Mafter, of the Academy at* Greenwich.

LONDON:

Printed for J. HOOKE, at the *Flower-de-Luce*, over-againft St. *Dunftan's* Church in *Fleet-ftreet.* M.DCC.XXX.

The title page of a 1730 English translation of Galileo's Two New Sciences. By this time, Galileo's ideas had spread throughout Europe.

mathematical style rapidly replaced Galileo's among scientists.

Like Galileo, Descartes was extremely critical of Aristotle. Unlike Galileo, he produced a work of philosophy to replace Aristotle. It was widely used in France and England for almost a century. Descartes was an innovator, but clearly of a different stamp from Galileo. Too much like Aristotle, he attempted to produce a philosophy that would explain everything. After Galileo's death, his work influenced men born long after 1600—two and three generations after him. His main scientific heirs lived in northwestern Europe.

During the 1500s, economic power shifted away from the Mediterranean to the Atlantic seaboard. Countries with overseas colonies plundered them for their riches—gold, spices, and furs. Spain had a brief burst of power but declined rapidly. France, England, and Holland soon took the lead. Their new economic power created an atmosphere in these countries that encouraged innovations in science and other fields.

In addition, Galileo's condemnation in 1633 had a withering effect on scientific activity in Italy. Where the Inquisition ruled, scientists felt constrained to be obedient. Although France was Catholic, the French tended to be masters in their own church. England and Holland were both Protestant.

In Holland, Christiaan Huygens came under Mersenne's influence. He studied the motions of bodies and used algebraic techniques to give a fully correct formula for the motion of pendulums. In astronomy, Huygens built improved telescopes that were good enough to resolve the rings of Saturn, which Galilean telescopes could not do. After 1666, Huygens became a leading member of the French Academy of Sciences.

The scientific star of the 1600s was undoubtedly Isaac Newton. Born in the English countryside in 1643, Newton attended Cambridge University in the 1660s. When he discovered mathematics, he plunged deeply into extending Descartes's analytic geometry. He also read Galileo's *Dialogue* in an English translation.

Using Descartes's geometry, Newton began to find ways to describe changing quantities. By 1665 he was developing calculus, which gives rules for expressing the rates of change of quantities. In 1666, Newton applied these rules to the acceleration of the moon toward the earth, and of an apple toward the earth. He supposed that these accelerations might be caused by a force emanating from the earth. Newton surmised that this force should diminish at greater distances, decreasing inversely as the square of the distance. For example, at 5 times the distance, the force should be 1/25 as much.

Newton knew from astronomy that the moon's distance is about 60 times the radius of the earth. Theoretically, the force and acceleration of the moon should be 1/3600 of the apple's. But when Newton used the numbers he knew, including a value for the apple's acceleration that he deduced from the *Dialogue,* his calculated result was 1/4300. Considering that amount too far from his theoretical expectation, he set the calculation aside. Twenty years later, using better data, he got 1/3600.

During this same period, Newton also found the rule for the pendulum, independently of Huygens. In 1669, Newton became professor of mathematics at Cambridge University. During the next 15 years he worked on optics and motion. He made the first reflecting telescope, which allowed gigantic improvements in observations compared to the telescopes of Galileo and Huygens.

In his studies of motion, Newton eventually turned to motions in the heavens. He applied his mathematical improvements of Galileo's rules to Kepler's elliptical orbits. With a burst of insight, he realized that elliptic orbits for planets about the sun would result from a force between them and the sun—with the force varying inversely as the square of the distance from the sun to the planet.

If the sun–planet force and the earth–apple/moon force both followed the same rule, could they be the same force? Newton decided they were. He invented the idea of the force of universal gravitation.

Newton's work completed Galileo's. For example, Newton showed that comets followed paths that were either long, narrow ellipses or parabolas. In either case, their orbits fitted his inverse square law of gravitational force. Newton also proposed that ocean tides come from the same force. They result from the differential force of gravity from the moon and the sun on the waters on opposite sides of the earth. Galileo's theory of the tides had not been correct.

Nonetheless, it should be clear that Galileo's work formed an important foundation for his successors. Beyond his telescopic discoveries, he put experimental measurements at the heart of physics. And his mathematical insight moved physics out of windy philosophy and into real science.

For 350 years Galileo's name has also evoked powerful social feelings. In the first century after his death, Galileo symbolized the fight for freedom in science against the arrayed forces of philosophy and religion—against the traditions of Aristotle and the militancy of Catholic Jesuits.

The process began while Galileo's body was barely cold in its crypt. In England, the poet John Milton complained about government censorship. In 1644, he wrote of visiting European countries that were being tyrannized by the Inquisition. Milton recalled in his essay *Areopagitica* that in Italy he had "found and visited the famous Galileo, grown old, a prisoner to the Inquisition for thinking in astronomy otherwise than the Franciscan and Dominican licensers thought."

Milton made Galileo a symbol of all victims of religious thought police, because he wanted to avoid having English authors receive similar treatment. During this time of civil war in England, Milton did help reduce the strict censorship of ideas.

In France, too, brilliant authors like Blaise Pascal and Voltaire invoked Galileo's name in their struggles for freedom of religion and of thought. In the 1650s, Pascal published an open letter to the Jesuits. He wrote:

> In vain did you obtain from Rome the decree against Galileo, condemning his opinion on the earth's motion. It will take more than that to prove that it keeps still. If there were consistent observations proving that the earth goes round, all the people in the world put together could not stop it turning, or themselves turning with it.

A hundred years later, Voltaire wrote:

> When the Inquisition's seven cardinals declared the theory that the earth moved was both heretical and absurd; and when the great Galileo, aged 70, had to ask pardon for being right, there seemed little chance of truth being received on earth.

These three authors all twisted Galileo's situation to serve their own purposes. Milton made it primarily a case of censorship. Pascal blamed the Jesuits, an accusation that can only be partly true. Voltaire oversimplified the case by making it seem that everyone knew Galileo was right. But in 1633, proof of the earth's motion was not secure. Galileo was right, but that is not why he was condemned. He was convicted mainly for being disobedient.

Through the 1600s and 1700s, traditional ideas still predominated. Church authorities needed little defense for their actions, since they continued in power. Only later, as the new ideas became widely accepted, did concerns arise about the correctness of the Inquisition's actions in 1616 and 1633.

The Church itself gradually changed with the times: 111 years after prohibiting the *Dialogue,* the Church allowed it to be published. However, a note in the preface stressed that the motion of the earth must be treated as a hypothesis. By the 1820s, the Church began to license books that treat-

ed the earth's motion as fact. The 1835 edition of the *Index of Prohibited Books* was the
first one not to prohibit books by
Copernicus, Kepler, and Galileo.

Yet Galileo's trial continues to echo
through the centuries into our own time.
Some defenders of science still accuse the
Catholic Church of committing a serious
error in condemning him. And the church
for its part feels unjustly burdened by actions
taken so long ago.

In 1979 Pope John Paul II decided to
investigate the whole issue to clear the air. In
a speech to a convention of scientists, he
declared that his church now agreed with
Galileo's view that religion and science both
contain truths that can never conflict. In
1981, the pope appointed a commission to
determine the Church's stand on Galileo today.

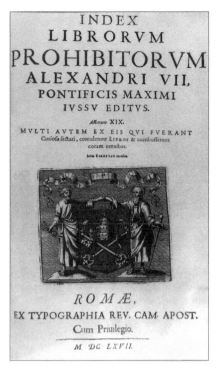

INDEX
LIBRORVM
PROHIBITORVM
ALEXANDRI VII,
PONTIFICIS MAXIMI
IVSSV EDITVS.

*Galileo's books were
kept on the Catholic
Church's* Index
Librorum Prohibitorum
*(Index of prohibited
books) until 1835.*

Following a number of studies, the commissioners
reported their findings at the end of 1992. They stated that
the sentence imposed on Galileo was not absolute but could
be rectified. In the light of new information, the Church
had in fact revised its stand on the motion of the earth back
in the 1800s.

The commission admitted that church authorities in
the 1600s had been wrong to turn facts of astronomy into
matters of religion. Nonetheless, given the state of knowledge at the time, they had acted in good faith. Viewed his-
torically, they could hardly have been expected to do other
than they did. Their errors in judgment led them to impose
much undue suffering on Galileo. "These mistakes must be
frankly recognized," the report concluded.

The Motion of Projectiles

In 1608, Galileo found a way to describe the path of an object thrown off at an angle by imagining the motion to be made up of a vertical and a horizontal component. Although he did some experimental work on this question, his mathematical analysis is more important.

Galileo described the motion of projectiles such as cannon shots. A good clue to his thought process occurs in the introduction he gave to the subject in his last book, *Two New Sciences* (1638):

> I imagine a moving object projected on a horizontal plane, assuming no impediments. If the plane were of infinite extent, the speed of this object would be constant. But if it ends, and has some elevation, the object (which I conceive being endowed with heaviness), going beyond the end of the plane, will have added to its uniform horizontal motion a downward tendency from its own heaviness. The resulting compound motion, which I call "projection," will have a definite shape. That is:
>
> *When a projectile is carried in a motion compounded from constant horizontal and naturally downward accelerated motions, it describes a parabolic line in its motion.*

Galileo showed, in effect, that a parabola (a curved line

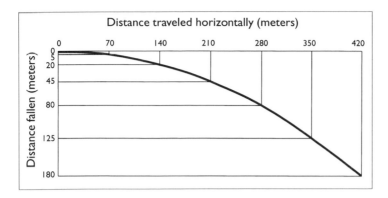

shaped like a jet of water from a fountain) has the same mathematical description as the combination of an accelerated vertical motion with a constant horizontal motion.

The diagram above shows the graph that results from such a combination. The normal acceleration of gravity is almost 10 m/sec^2. The distances fallen increase in proportion to the square of the elapsed time. The table shows distances fallen combined with a horizontal speed of 70 m/s. The diagram is a graph in space of the distance values.

Time (s)	Time^2 (s^2)	Vertical distance (m)	Horizontal distance (m)
0	0	0	0
1	1	5	70
2	4	20	140
3	9	45	210
4	16	80	280
5	25	125	350
6	36	180	420

The mathematics is more complicated for slanting projections, yet projectiles fired at an angle still follow a parabolic path, as shown above. However, these paths do not take account of air resistance or the curvature of the earth. Real projectiles follow a somewhat different path. Isaac Newton worked out the details in the 1680s.

Measuring Motions

Galileo watched a ball gather speed as it rolled down a gent-ly inclined plane. The ball, about an inch in diameter, rolled in a grooved board about six feet long. Repeatedly Galileo marked the successive positions the ball reached while he chanted a regular rhythm. Once he had become systemati-cally precise, he measured the distances the ball had rolled in each equal interval of time. Using the first distance as a unit, he found that the distances traveled in eight equal times fol-lowed the sequence 1, 3, 5, 7, 9, 11, 13, 15.

Shortly after performing this experiment, Galileo real-ized that the successive sums of these numbers were the squares of the elapsed times from the start. The sums are 1, 4 (that is, 1+3), 9 (1+3+5), 16 (1+3+5+7), 25 (1+3+5+7+9), 36, 49, and 64, which are the squares of the numbers from 1 to 8. This means that the distances the ball traversed from rest were in proportion to the squares of the elapsed times.

While chanting the beats of a song can produce very nearly equal time intervals, it does not measure varying time intervals. Galileo devised a water clock that could measure time to better than a hundredth of a second. He arranged to start and stop a fine flow of water; he then collected and weighed the amount of water that had flowed.

Galileo measured the weight of water in grains. A grain is 1/480 of an ounce. For the rate of flow of water he used, he established a unit of time that is about 1/100 second. The unit of length that he used was very nearly 1 millimeter. In these examples taken from Galileo's notes, we have converted his measurements to seconds and meters.

Time from start	Distance in unit time	Distance from start
0	0	0
1	1	1
2	3	4
3	5	9
4	7	16
5	9	25
6	11	36
7	13	49
8	15	64

Galileo first timed a swinging pendulum. Using two identical pendulums, he could show that each complete swing (over and back) takes the same time. The swing from release to the vertical takes a quarter of the time for a complete swing.

Galileo used his water clock to time the swings of pendulums of various lengths. He may have timed several full swings and then calculated the time for a quarter swing. Stopping and starting the clock precisely takes considerable practice. Galileo found the time for a pendulum 0.818 meters long to be 0.45 seconds; one 1.636 meters long took 0.64 seconds.

Length of pendulum (m)	Time for a quarter swing (seconds)	Square of the time	Length/time^2
0.818	0.45	0.203	4.03
1.636	0.64	0.410	3.99
[3.272]	[0.90]	[0.810]	[4.04]

A pendulum of double the length takes $\sqrt{2}$ times longer for a quarter swing. That should mean that it would take four times the length to get double the time. In the table on the bottom of page 115, the numbers in the third line are calculated, not measured. The length is double the length just above it, and the time is $\sqrt{2}$ times the time above it. They show that a pendulum four times longer than the first one will take twice as long to swing. The fourth column shows that for each pendulum, the length divided by the square of the time gives almost the same number in each case.

Expressed in words, the relation is that the time of swing of a pendulum is proportional to the square root of its length. To put it another way, the length is proportional to the square of the time. As with the inclined plane, a length varies in proportion to the *square* of time.

Galileo next turned to measuring the times of vertical falls. For distances of more than a couple of meters, the starting and stopping of the water clock at the right moments becomes difficult. When several measurements also appeared to relate distances to the squares of the times, Galileo related vertical fall to the pendulum. For a fall through a height equal to the length of a pendulum, he found that the time was very close to 0.900 times as much. ($0.900 = 2\sqrt{2}/\pi$; the π coming from the fact that the pendulum swings on the arc of a circle.)

You can check Galileo's work by using the formulas found in physics textbooks. For a pendulum of length d, the time T for a quarter swing is given by the formula

$$T = \frac{\pi}{2}\sqrt{\frac{d}{g}}$$

where g, the acceleration of gravity, is 9.8 m/s^2.

You can apply this formula to the numbers given in the table.

For a vertical free fall of distance *d* in time *t*, the formula is

$$d = \frac{g}{2}t^2$$

This formula can be rearranged to give time in terms of distance:

$$t = \sqrt{\frac{2d}{g}}$$

Now, if the body falls a distance equal to the length of the pendulum, then

$$\frac{t}{T} = \frac{\sqrt{\frac{2d}{g}}}{\frac{\pi}{2}\sqrt{\frac{d}{g}}} = \frac{\sqrt{2}}{\pi/2} = \frac{2\sqrt{2}}{\pi}$$

Galileo gave this number in his notes as the fraction 850/942. With your calculator you can find that Galileo's value differs from the modern theoretical value by less than 0.23 percent.

As a final check on the relations he was developing, Galileo made two large tests. A pendulum 9.25 meters long took 1.53 seconds to swing to the vertical, and an object fell 45.25 meters in 3.05 seconds.

You should realize that Galileo always gave his results as ratios. He did not use algebra and never expressed the relations as formulas like those above. However, you could use those formulas to see how closely his final tests match our modern calculations.

Also, because Galileo used ratios rather than formulas, he did not ever give an explicit value for *g*, the acceleration of gravity. These measurements and calculations show the earliest results that Galileo obtained in his new science of motion.

CHRONOLOGY

February 15, 1564
Galileo born in Pisa (in Tuscany)

1574–81
Educated at Florence and Vallombrosa

November 1581
Enrolls in University of Pisa, intended for medical degree

early 1583
Begins to study math in preference to regular studies

May 1585
Leaves university without a degree

November 1589–May 1592
Professor of mathematics at University of Pisa; becomes critical of Aristotle's teachings on motion

December 1592–August 1610
Professor of mathematics at University of Padua (Venetian Republic); sires three illegitimate children

1596–99
Adapts and improves compass for gunnery calculations

November 1602
Letter to Guidobaldo on long pendulums

October 1604
Has pendulum law and times-squared law of fall

1605–08
Work culminates in finding speed of fall proportional to time, and parabolic trajectory of projectiles

August 1609
Produces first nine-power telescope

December 1609
Determines that lunar surface is rough and mountainous

January 1610
  Discovers moons of Jupiter

March 1610
  Starry Messenger published in Venice

September 1610
  Moves to Florence in employ of Grand Duke of Tuscany

April 1611
  Elected to Lincean Academy in Rome

June 1612
  Bodies in Water published in Florence

May 1613
  Letters on Sunspots published in Rome

February 1616
  Cautioned by Roman Inquisition to abandon
  Copernicanism

October 1623
  The Assayer published in Rome

April–June 1624
  Visits old friend in Rome, now Pope Urban VIII; soon
  begins to write *Dialogue*

February 21, 1632
  Dialogue published in Florence

June 22, 1633
  Condemned by Inquisition for suspicion of heresy

December 1633
  Returns to home in Arcetri

June 1638
  Two New Sciences published in Leyden, Holland

January 8, 1642
  Galileo dies in Arcetri

The Life and Times of Galileo

Biagioli, Mario. *Galileo, Courtier: The Practice of Science in the Culture of Absolutism*. Chicago: University of Chicago Press, 1993.

Blackwell, Richard J. *Galileo, Bellarmine, and the Church*. South Bend, Ind.: University of Notre Dame Press, 1991.

Brecht, Bertolt. *The Life of Galileo*. New York: Grove, 1966.

Campanella, Thomas. *A Defense of Galileo, 1616*. Trans. R. J. Blackwell. South Bend, Ind.: University of Notre Dame Press, 1994.

De Santillana, Giorgio. *The Crime of Galileo*. Chicago: University of Chicago Press, 1955.

Drake, Stillman. *Discoveries and Opinions of Galileo*. Garden City, N.Y.: Doubleday, 1957.

———. *Galileo at Work*. Chicago: University of Chicago Press, 1978.

———. *Galileo*. New York: Oxford University Press, 1980.

———. *Cause, Experiment, and Science: A Galilean Dialogue Incorporating a New Translation of Galileo's Discourse on Things That Rest upon Water or Move in It (1612)*. Chicago: University of Chicago Press, 1981.

———. *Telescopes, Tides, and Tactics: A Galilean Dialogue about the "Starry Messenger" and "Systems of the World."* Chicago: University of Chicago Press, 1983.

———. *Galileo: Pioneer Scientist*. Toronto: University of Toronto Press, 1989.

———. "Galileo's Discovery of the Law of Free Fall." *Scientific American* 228, no. 5 (1973): 84–92.

———. "The Role of Music in Galileo's Experiments." *Scientific American* 232, no. 6 (1975): 98–104.

———. "Galileo and the First Mechanical Computing Device." *Scientific American* 234, no. 4 (1976): 104–13.

————. "Newton's Apple and Galileo's *Dialogue*." *Scientific American* 243, no. 2 (1980): 151–56.

Drake, Stillman and C. T. Kowal. "Galileo's Sighting of Neptune." *Scientific American* 243, no. 6 (1980): 74–81.

Drake, Stillman and J. MacLachlan. "Galileo's Discovery of the Parabolic Trajectory." *Scientific American* 232, no. 3 (1975): 102–10.

Fantoli, Annibale. *Galileo: For Copernicanism and for the Church*. Vatican City: Vatican Observatory Publications, 1994.

Feldhay, Rivka. *Galileo and the Church: Political Inquisition or Critical Dialogue?* Cambridge: Cambridge University Press, 1995.

Finocchiaro, Maurice A. *The Galileo Affair: A Documentary History*. Berkeley: University of California Press, 1989.

————. *Galileo on the World Systems: A New Abridged Translation and Guide*. Berkeley: University of California Press, 1997.

Galilei, Galileo. *Dialogue concerning the Two Chief World Systems—Ptolemaic and Copernican, 1632*. Trans. S. Drake. Berkeley: University of California Press, 1967.

Galilei, Galileo. *Two New Sciences: Including Centers of Gravity and Force of Percussion, 1638*. Trans. S. Drake. Toronto: Wall and Thompson, 1989.

Gingerich, Owen. "The Galileo Affair." *Scientific American* 247, no. 2 (1982): 132–43.

Langford, Jerome J. *Galileo, Science and the Church*. Ann Arbor: University of Michigan Press, 1966.

Pedersen, Olaf. *Galileo and the Council of Trent*. Rev. ed. Vatican City: Vatican Observatory Publications, 1991.

Sharratt, Michael. *Galileo: Decisive Innovator*. Oxford: Blackwell, 1994.

Smith, Gerald. *Galileo: A Dramatised Life*. London: Janus, 1995.

Stavis, Barrie. *Lamp at Midnight: A Play about Galileo*. South Brunswick: A. S. Barnes, 1966.

Physics and the History of Science

Agassi, Joseph. *The Continuing Revolution: A History of Physics from the Greeks to Einstein.* New York: McGraw-Hill, 1968.

Alioto, Anthony M. *A History of Western Science.* Englewood Cliffs, N.J.: Prentice-Hall, 1987.

Charon, Jean. *Cosmology: Theories of the Universe.* New York: World University Library, 1970.

Chartrand, Mark R. *Skyguide: A Field Guide for Amateur Astronomers.* New York: Golden Press, 1982.

Cohen, I. Bernard. *The Birth of a New Physics.* Rev. ed. New York: W. W. Norton, 1985.

Crowe, Michael J. *Theories of the World from Antiquity to the Copernican Revolution.* New York: Dover, 1990.

Gingerich, Owen. *The Great Copernicus Chase and Other Adventures in Astronomical History.* Cambridge, Mass.: Sky Publishing, 1992.

Kearney, Hugh. *Science and Change, 1500–1700.* New York: McGraw-Hill, 1971.

Kuhn, Thomas S. *The Copernican Revolution: Planetary Astronomy in the Development of Western Thought.* New York: Random House, 1959.

MacLachlan, James. *Children of Prometheus: A History of Science and Technology.* Toronto: Wall and Emerson, 1989.

Marks, John. *Science and the Making of the Modern World.* New York: Heinemann, 1983.

Moore, Patrick. *The Great Astronomical Revolution: 1543–1687.* London: Albion, 1994.

Morrison, Philip and Phylis. *The Ring of Truth.* New York: Vintage, 1989.

Segrè, Emilio. *From Falling Bodies to Radio Waves: Classical Physicists and Their Discoveries.* San Francisco: W. H. Freeman, 1984.

Smith, Alan G. R. *Science and Society in the Sixteenth and Seventeenth Centuries.* London: Thames and Hudson, 1972.

Westfall, Richard S. *The Construction of Modern Science: Mechanisms and Mechanics.* Cambridge: Cambridge University Press, 1977.

INDEX

Archivio Segreto Vaticano: 96; Art Resource, New York: 30, 49, 83, 97; Biblioteca Accademia dei Lincei Corsiniana di Roma: 57; British Library: 106; Istituto e Museo di Storia della Scienza, Florence: 37, 48; Library of Congress: 2, 10, 17, 19, 26, 28, 46, 71, 77, 81, 102, 111; Lilly Library, University of Indiana: 33; diagrams by Gary Tong: 15, 47, 64, 88, 89, 99, 113; University of Toronto, Fisher Rare Book Library: 22, 44, 54, 66, 68, 87, 91, 93, 100

James MacLachlan is emeritus professor of history at Ryerson Polytechnic University in Toronto. He is the author of *Children of Prometheus: A History of Science and Technology* and *Matter and Energy: Foundations of Modern Physics,* as well as a number of articles on Galileo and Mersenne.

Owen Gingerich is Professor of Astronomy and of the History of Science at the Harvard–Smithsonian Center for Astrophysics in Cambridge, Massachusetts. The author of more than 400 articles and reviews, he has also written *The Great Copernicus Chase and Other Adventures in Astronomical History* and *The Eye of Heaven: Ptolemy, Copernicus, Kepler.*